Name ________________________________

Cut and paste the shape that is just

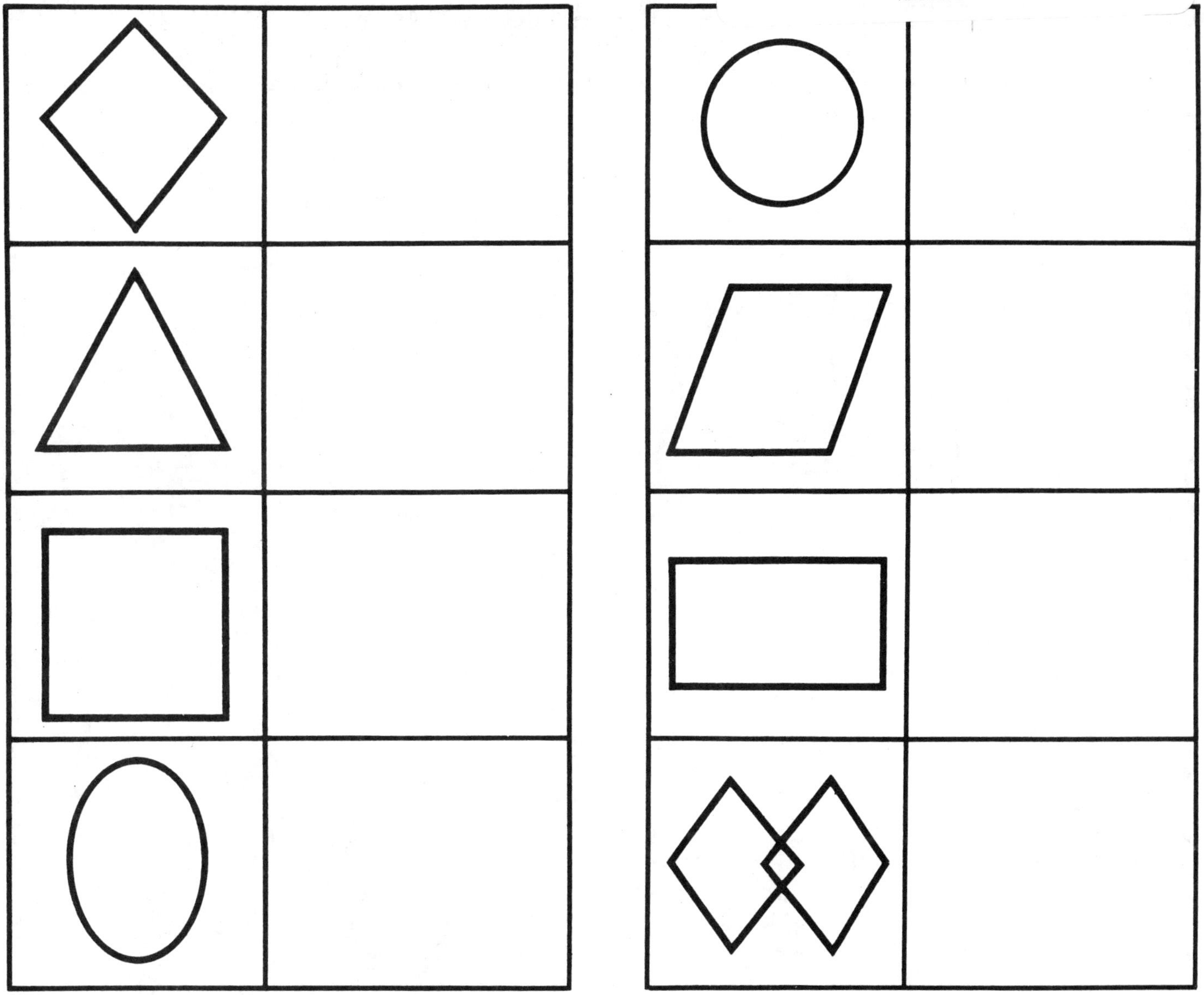

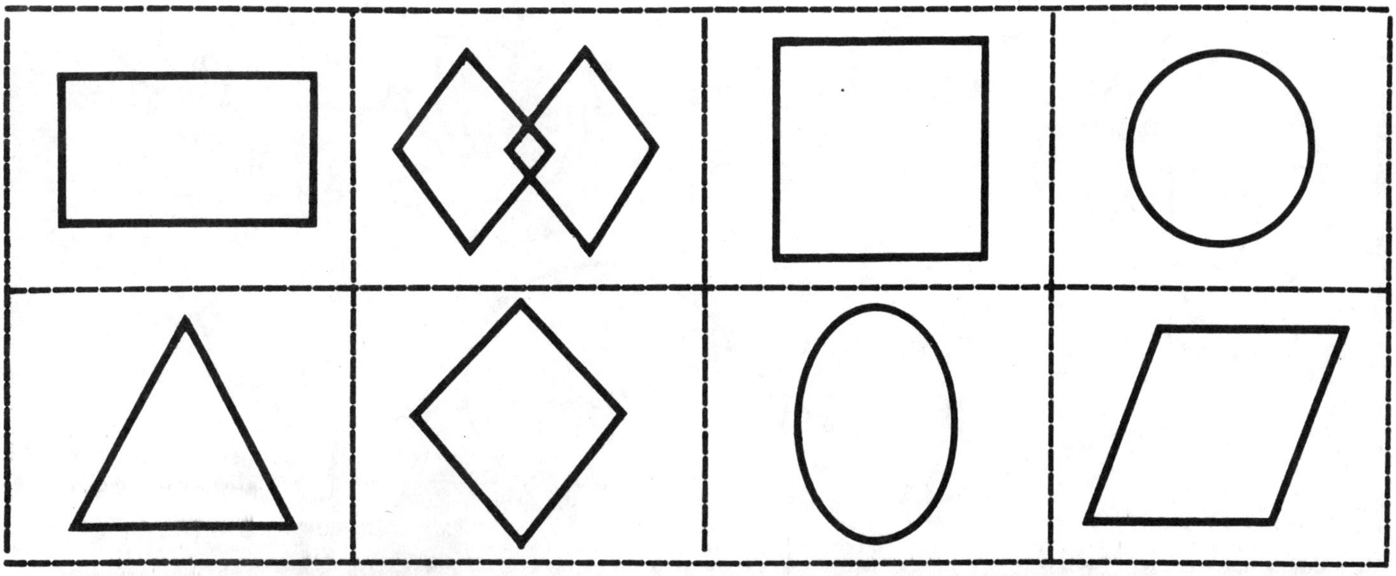

Name ______________________________

Look at the picture. With a brown crayon, color all the animals that are alike. Color the rest of the picture in your favorite colors.

Name ______________________________

Mrs. Bunny has lots of children. It's hard to tell them apart. Color the bunnies that are different.

Name ____

Cut out each fish and paste it next to its twin.

Name ____

The bears in the forest are having a party. Color the bears that are different.

Name ______________________________

Look at Farmer Fred's hens. Color the hens that are alike.

Name ______________________________

Look at the road. Color the cars that are alike.

Name ______________________________

Cut out the boats below. Paste them in the right places.

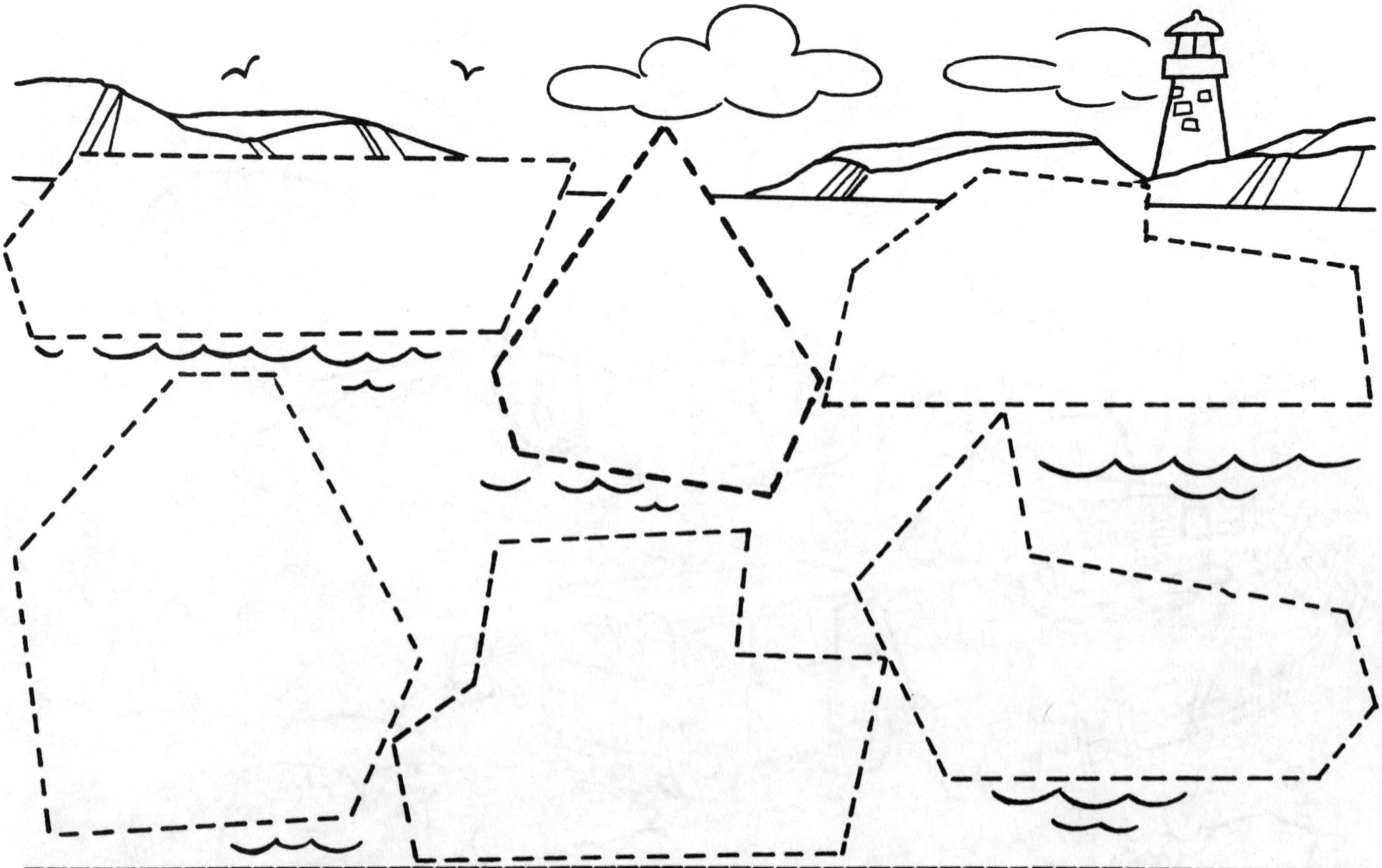

Name ______________________________

It's a windy day! Color all the kites that are different.

Name ______________________________

Cut and paste each twin.

Name ____

Cut and paste each face next to its twin.

Name ______________________________

Color the flowers that are different.

Name ______________________________

It's a snowy day. Circle all the snowflakes that are alike.
Color the picture.

Name ____________________

Color the cards that are alike in each row.

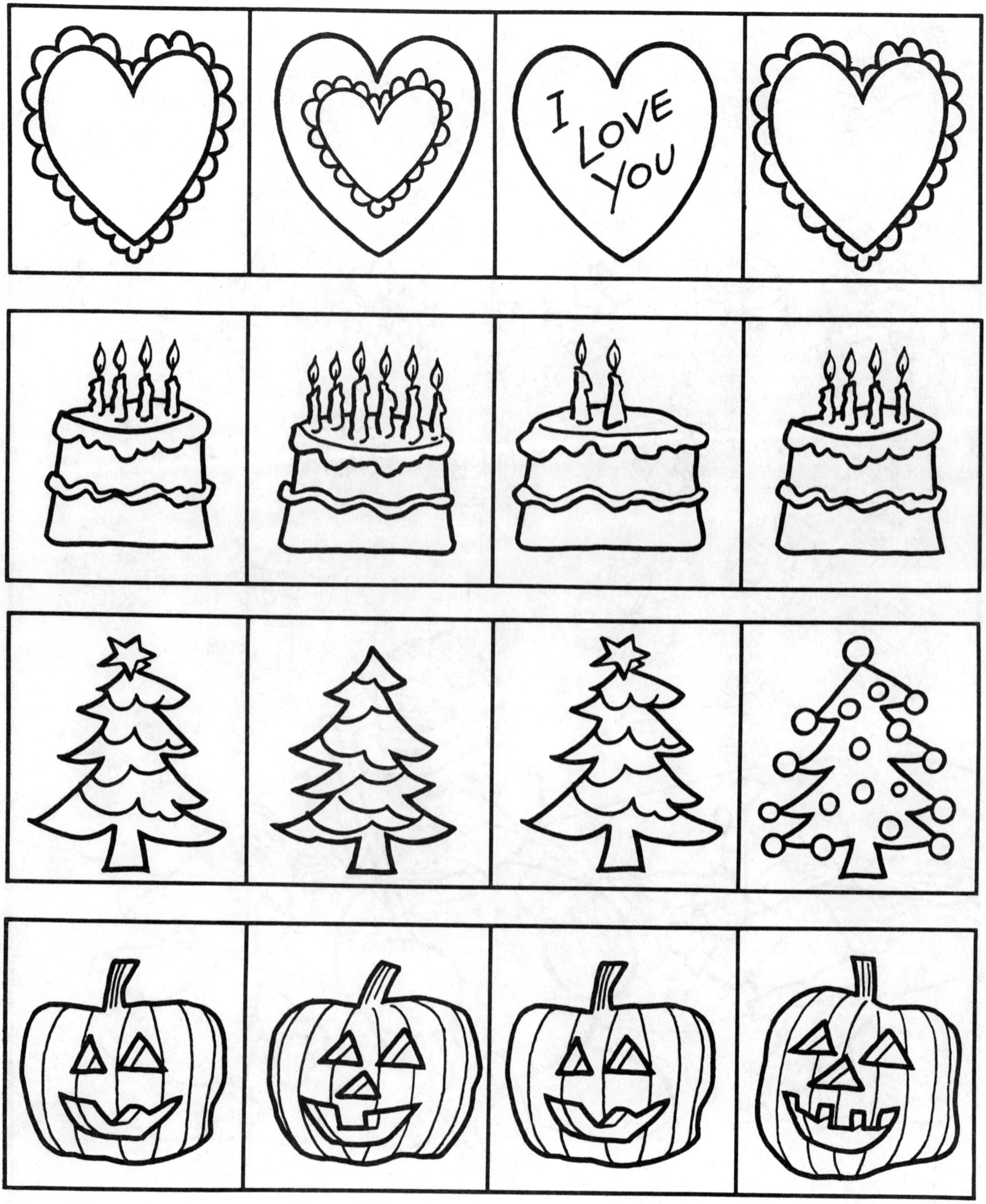

Name ______________________________

Cut and paste the pictures that are alike.

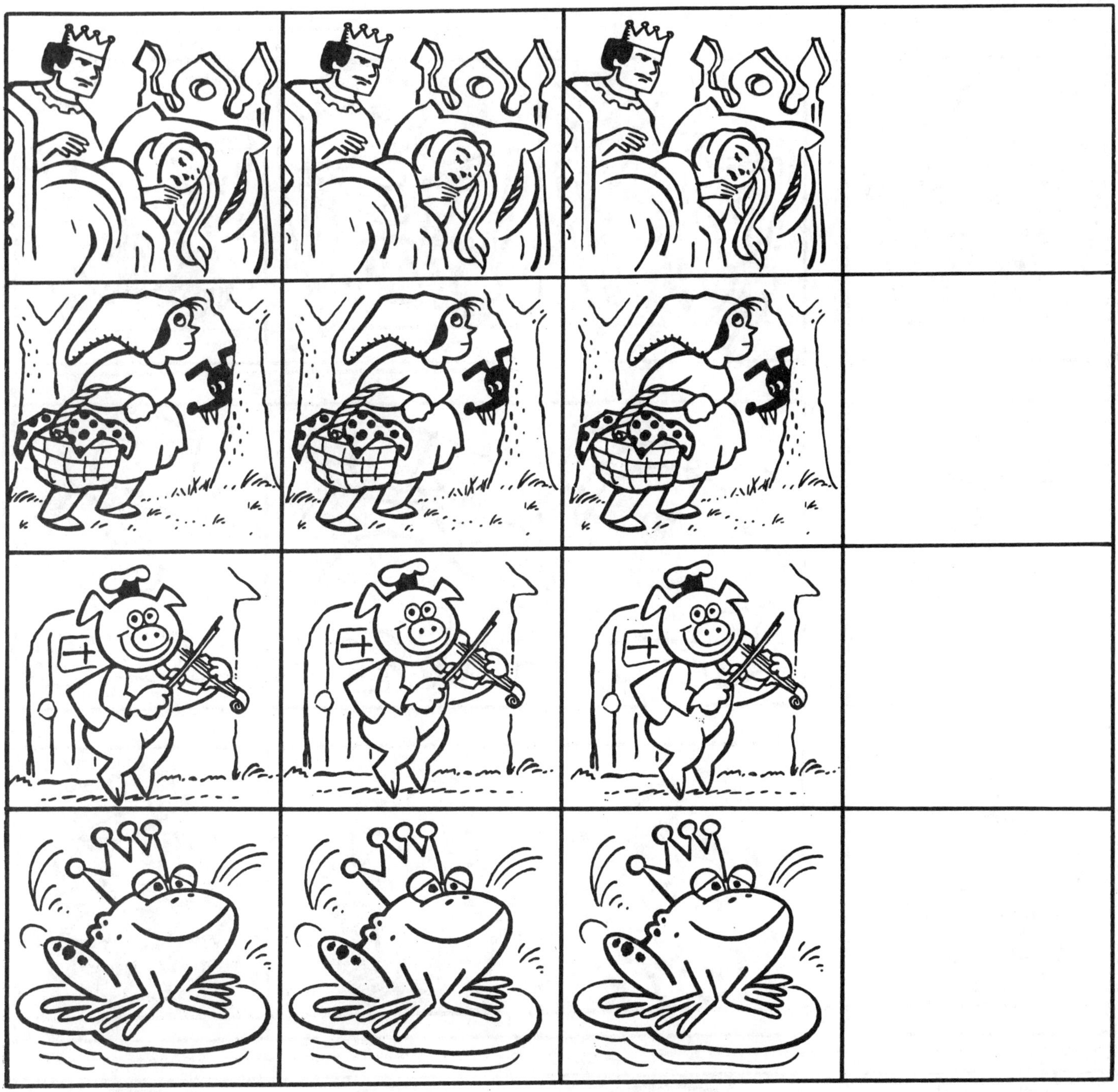

Name ______________________________

Look at each row. Color the pictures that are different from the first one.

Name ____

Ann wants to give her friend a set of her vacation pictures. Cut and paste each picture next to the one that is alike.

Name ______________________________

Color the vegetables and trees that are alike.

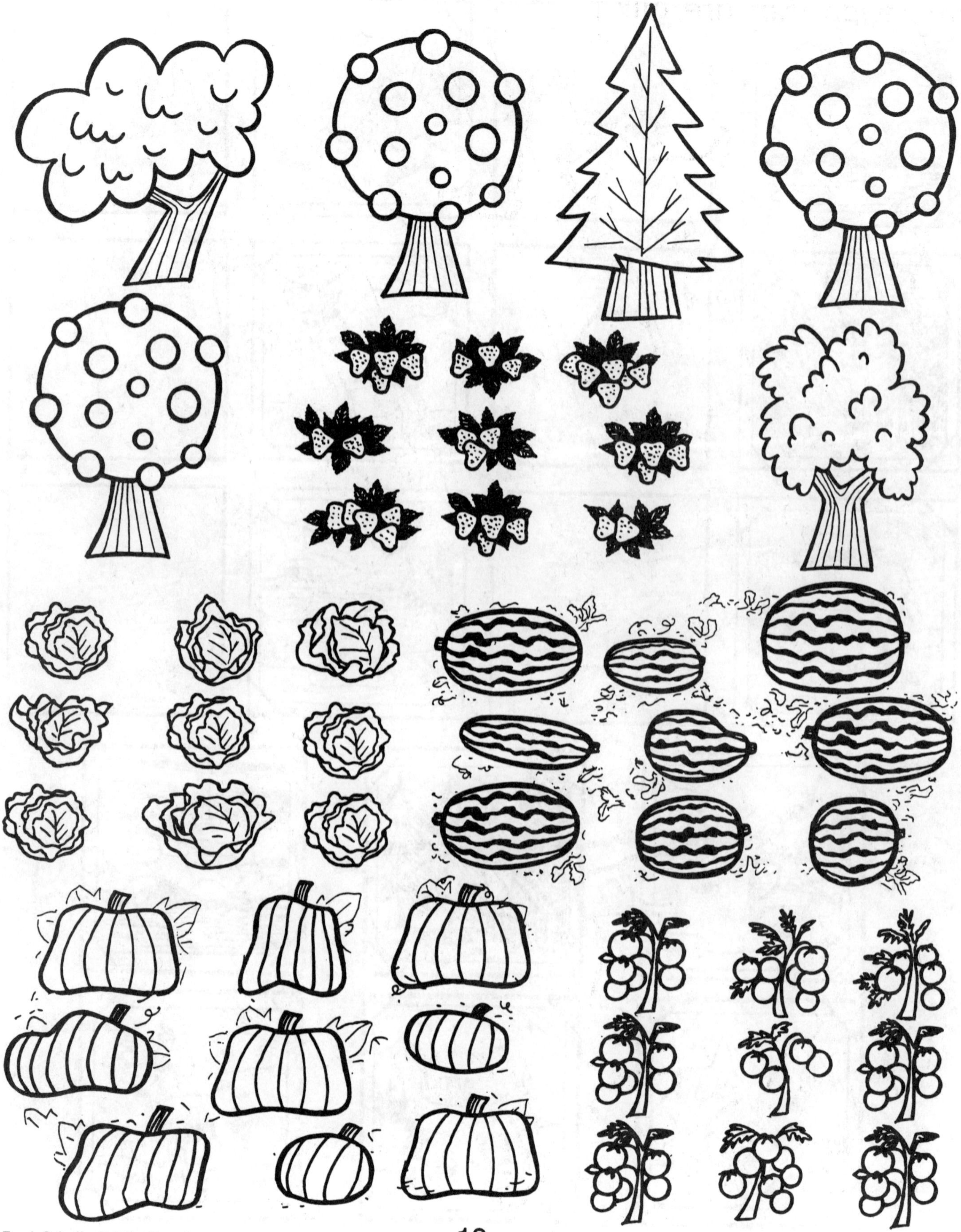

Name ______________________________

It's raining cats and dogs! Color all the cats, dogs and umbrellas that are alike.

Name ______________________________

Color everything that is alike in each row.

Name ________________________________ Skill: Visual perception—short vowel **a** words

Word Box			
apple	cat	fan	hat
map	bat	glass	tack
clam	flag	candle	lamb

Find the pictures of the words from the Word Box. Color them.

Name ______________________________ Skill: Visual perception—short vowel **e** words

Word Box			
bed	dress	hen	net
bell	egg	jet	pen
desk	fence	nest	web

Find the pictures of the words from the Word Box. Color them.

Name ______________________________ Skill: Visual perception—short vowel **i** words

Word Box			
chick	king	pig	whistle
fish	milk	pin	wig
hill	mitt	ship	zipper

Find the pictures of the words from the Word Box. Color them.

Name ______________________________ Skill: Visual perception—short vowel **u** words

Word Box			
bug	duck	hut	rug
bus	bun	nut	sun
cup	jug	umbrella	truck

Find the pictures of the words from the Word Box. Color them.

Name ______________________________ Skill: Visual perception—long vowel **i** words

Word Box			
bride	five	tire	nine
file	ice	vine	prize
fire	kite	mice	wire

Find the pictures of the words from the Word Box. Color them.

Name ____ Skill: Visual perception—numbers 11-20

Find the numerals from 11-20. Color them orange.
Color the rest of the picture.

Name ______________________________ Skill: Visual perception—rhyming words

Word Box

man	hat	pop	pet
fan	cat	mop	net
pan	mat	top	jet

Find the pictures of the words from the Word Box. Color them.

Name ____________________

Skill: Visual perception—farm animals

Word Box

pig	horse	rabbit	goose
hen	dog	sheep	goat
cow	cat	duck	turkey

Find the pictures of the words from the Word Box. Color them.

Name ____ Skill: Visual perception—compound words

Word Box

baseball	doghouse	popcorn	spaceship
beehive	football	sailboat	starfish
butterfly	paintbrush	schoolhouse	sunflower

Find the pictures of the words from the Word Box. Color them.

Name ____ Skill: Visual perception — compound words

Word Box

basketball	clothespin	overalls	rainbow
bulldog	handcuff	pancakes	watermelon
clipboard	haystack	peanuts	windmill

Find the pictures of the words from the Word Box. Color them.

Name ______________________________ Skill: Visual perception—consonant blends

Word Box			
swing	slide	skunk	spoon
sled	swan	spider	skis
sweater	sleeping bag	skate	space suit

Find the pictures of the words from the Word Box. Color them.

Name ______________________ Skill: Completing sentences, Following directions

Read the sentences to find out how to color the picture.

bird rabbit sand sun

1. The yellow ______________ was in the sky.

2. The ______________ has a green pail.

3. The brown rabbit sat in the ______________ .

4. A blue ______________ was on the log.

5. The brown log was in the ______________ .

6. A red crab was in the yellow ______________ .

Name ________________________________ Skill: Completing sentences, Following directions

Read the sentences to find out how to color the picture.

box	dog	grass	wagon

1. An orange hat was on the ____________.

2. The brown dog was on the ____________.

3. Three yellow eggs are in a ____________.

4. The red wagon is on the ____________.

5. A brown hen sat in the ____________.

6. The black box is on the green ____________.

Name ________________________________ Skill: Completing sentences, Following directions

Read the sentences to find out how to color the picture.

grass hat turtle mouse

1. A black ________________ was on the rabbit.

2. The brown rabbit was on the ________________.

3. A black ________________ sat on the turtle.

4. A red hat was on the green ________________.

5. The turtle was on the green ________________.

6. A red bug was on the ________________.

Name ________________________ Skill: Completing sentences, Following directions

Read the sentences to find out how to color the picture.

box cat dog grass

1. The ________________ has a red kite.

2. The orange ________________ sat in a chair.

3. The blue chair was on the ________________.

4. A black ________________ sat in the box.

5. The yellow box was on the green ________________.

6. A brown mouse was on the ________________.

Name ______________________

Skill: Completing sentences,
Following directions

Read the sentences to find out how to color the picture.

balloon	book	box	grass

1. The mouse has a red ______________.

2. The brown mouse sat on a ______________.

3. The blue box was on the ______________.

4. The orange cat sat on the ______________.

5. The dog has a yellow ______________.

6. The black dog sat on the green ______________.

Name ______________________ Skill: Completing sentences, Following directions

Read the sentences to find out how to color the picture.

box	grass	rabbit	sun

1. The red hat was on the ______________.

2. The brown rabbit was on the ______________.

3. A big, black bear was on the ______________.

4. A brown mouse sat on a ______________.

5. The blue box was on the green ______________.

6. The yellow ______________ was in the sky.

Name ______________________ Skill: Completing sentences, Following directions

Read the sentences to find out how to color the picture.

book box chair grass

1. The dog has a red ______________________.

2. The black dog sat on a ______________________.

3. The blue chair was on the ______________________.

4. The orange bird was on the ______________________.

5. The black box was on the green ______________________.

6. The brown snake was in the ______________________.

Name ______________________________ Skill: Completing sentences, Following directions

Read the sentences to find out how to color the picture.

bear	bee	box	grass

1. The black rabbit hid in the ______________________.

2. A yellow duck sat in the ______________________.

3. The orange box was on the ______________________.

4. A blue hat was on the brown ______________________.

5. The bear was on the green ______________________.

6. The yellow ______________________ flew up and up.

Name ______________________ Skill: Completing sentences, Following directions

Read the sentences to find out how to color the picture.

box	fish	grass	jar

1. The red flag was in the ______________.
2. The orange cat was in the ______________.
3. The blue box was on the ______________.
4. A red ______________ was in the jar.
5. A yellow duck looked into the ______________.
6. The jar is on the green ______________.

Name ______________________ Skill: Completing sentences, Following directions

Read the sentences to find out how to color the picture.

bee	box	duck	grass	rabbit

1. The yellow ______________________ flew.
2. The black mouse sat on a ______________________.
3. The yellow duck was on the ______________________.
4. A blue hat was on the ______________________.
5. The brown rabbit sat on a ______________________.
6. The red box was on the green ______________________.

Name ____________________ Skill: Completing sentences, Following directions

Read the sentences to find out how to color the picture.

1. The brown hen sat on the ____________.

2. The blue star is on the ____________.

3. The red pig sat in a ____________.

4. The yellow box is on the ____________.

5. The red hat is on the black ____________.

6. The dog was on the green ____________.

Name ______________________________ Skill: Completing sentences, Following directions

Read the sentences to find out how to color the picture.

ball	boat	pond

1. The yellow duck sat in a ____________________.

2. The brown cat sat in a ____________________.

3. The boat was in the blue ____________________.

4. A red flag was on the green ____________________.

5. The seal has an orange ____________________.

6. The black seal swam in the ____________________.

Name ______________________________

Skill: Completing sentences, Following directions

Read the sentences to find out how to color the picture.

bear box dog mouse

1. The yellow hat was on a ____________________.

2. The brown ____________________ was on a red ball.

3. The ____________________ has an orange balloon .

4. The black mouse sat on a ____________________.

5. The brown dog sat on a ____________________.

6. Two red stars are on a blue ____________________.

Name ______________________

Skill: Completing sentences, Following directions

Read the sentences to find out how to color the picture.

1. The red hat is on the ______________________.

2. The ______________________ has a green pail.

3. The orange cat sat in the ______________________.

4. The ______________________ has a red fish.

5. The black bird is on a brown ______________________.

6. The rock is in the yellow ______________________.

Name ______________________________

Skill: Completing sentences, Following directions

Read the sentences to find out how to color the picture.

box	dog	grass	hat	turtle

1. The red bug sat on the ______________.

2. A blue hat was on the ______________.

3. The brown dog got down from a ______________.

4. A black mouse sat on the ______________.

5. The green turtle was on the ______________.

6. The yellow box was on the green ______________.

Name ______________________

Skill: Completing sentences, Following directions

Read the sentences to find out how to color the picture.

grass	pond	sun	turtle

1. The yellow duck swam in the ______________.

2. The red fish jumped in the blue ______________.

3. The yellow ______________ was in the sky.

4. The red bug sat on the black ______________.

5. The turtle was on the green ______________.

6. The brown dog was on the ______________.

Name ______________________

Skill: Completing sentences, Following directions

Read the sentences to find out how to color the picture.

ball can seal wagon

1. The brown dog hid in a ______________________.

2. The black can is in a red ______________________.

3. The yellow balloon is on the ______________________.

4. A green hat is on the ______________________.

5. The black seal has a red ______________________.

6. The ______________________ is on a blue box.

Name ______________________________ Skill: Completing sentences, Following directions

Read the sentences to find out how to color the picture.

dog	grass	hat	turtle

1. The green turtle was on the ____________.
2. The black rabbit sat on the ____________.
3. A red bug sat on a blue ____________.
4. A yellow duck was on the ____________.
5. The brown dog was on the ____________.
6. The dog was on the green ____________.

Name ______________________ Skill: Completing sentences, Following directions

Read the sentences to find out how to color the picture.

1. A black mouse sat in a blue ____________.

2. The hat was on the green ____________.

3. The yellow duck was on the ____________.

4. The orange ____________ sat in the wagon.

5. The ____________ has a red balloon.

6. The red wagon was on the ____________.

Name ______________________________

Skill: Completing sentences, Following directions

Read the sentences to find out how to color the picture.

balloon	bear	bee	box

1. The black cat has an orange ______________.

2. The cat sat in a blue ______________.

3. A blue hat is on a brown ______________.

4. The ______________ has a red jar.

5. The ______________ sat in the green grass.

6. The yellow ______________ flew in the sky.

What is the best paper to make kites from?

1. Find and color these words **yellow**.

chops	cheer	chimp
cheese	chill	it

c	c	h	o	p	s
h	c	h	e	e	r
e	f	l	y	i	t
e	c	h	i	l	l
s	p	a	p	e	r
e	c	h	i	m	p

2. Now, find the mystery answer. Color it **red** and write it on the line below.

What's the best thing to have?

1. Find and color these words **orange**.

horses	drive	fork	soap
	sleep	smoke	

f	s	l	e	e	p
o	d	r	i	v	e
r	a	s	o	a	p
k	s	m	o	k	e
f	r	i	e	n	d
h	o	r	s	e	s

2. Now, find the mystery answer. Color it **purple** and write it on the line below.

What kind of dog has no tail?

1. Find and color these words **brown**.

cheese	bun	butter	shop
man	at	he	new

b	u	t	t	e	r
s	h	o	p	a	m
h	n	e	w	a	a
e	h	o	t	t	n
c	h	e	e	s	e
b	u	n	d	o	g

2. Now, find the mystery answer. Color it **yellow** and write it on the line below.

What is a zebra after it is five years old?

1. Find and color these words **blue**.

feet	dog	up	get
in	color	leg	out

f	e	e	t	g	l
s	i	x	u	e	e
d	o	g	p	t	g
i	y	e	a	r	s
n	c	o	l	o	r
o	u	t	o	l	d

2. Now, find the mystery answer. Color it **yellow** and write it on the line below.

What is red and eats rocks?

1. Find and color these words **yellow**.

duck	I	my	day
sky	blue	slow	do

s	a	b	l	u	e
k	d	r	e	d	s
y	o	d	a	y	l
r	o	c	k	m	o
d	u	c	k	y	w
l	e	a	t	e	r

2. Now, find the mystery answer. Color it **red** and write it on the line below.

____

What belongs only to you?

1. Find and color these words **yellow**.

shoes	card	not	yes
hands	blue	book	

b o o k h s

y o u r a h

c b y n n o

a l e o d e

r u s t s s

d e n a m e

Now, find the mystery answer. Color it **purple** and write it on the line below.

What has legs but cannot walk?

1. Find and color these words **red**.

five	light	twenty	chair
	lamps	night	

t	w	e	n	t	y
a	l	a	m	p	s
f	c	h	a	i	r
i	t	a	b	l	e
v	l	i	g	h	t
e	n	i	g	h	t

2. Now, find the mystery answer. Color it **blue** and write it on the line below

What is the best thing to put into a pie?

1. Find and color these words **yellow**.

nose	**arm**	**mouth**
hands	**bones**	**belly**

a	m	o	u	t	h
r	y	o	u	r	h
m	n	o	s	e	a
t	e	e	t	h	n
b	o	n	e	s	d
b	e	l	l	y	s

2. Now, find the mystery answer. Color it **green** and write it on the line below.

What runs but never walks?

1. Find and color these words **orange**.

wagon	kite	dogs	bus
baby	girl	ant	rain

w	k	r	a	i	n
a	i	d	o	g	s
g	t	g	i	r	l
o	e	b	a	b	y
n	w	a	t	e	r
b	u	s	a	n	t

2. Now, find the mystery answer. Color it **green** and write it on the line below.

What dog keeps the best time?

1. Find and color these words **purple**.

spell	read	add	go
math	lunch	wait	

r	e	a	d	g	o
m	a	w	a	i	t
a	l	u	n	c	h
t	w	a	t	c	h
h	s	p	e	l	l
d	o	g	a	d	d

2. Now, find the mystery answer. Color it **orange** and write it on the line below.

My hair is falling out. What can I get to keep it in?

1. Find and color these words **blue**.

spot	tail	if	socks
eggs	wheel	tin	

s	p	o	t	a	e
w	h	e	e	l	g
p	a	p	e	r	g
t	t	a	i	l	s
i	i	f	b	a	g
n	s	o	c	k	s

2. Now, find the mystery answer. Color it **yellow** and write it on the line below.

What has a head and a tail but no body?

1. Find and color these words **orange**.

trap	ape	pie	trains	
face	if	am	dark	day

f	d	a	y	t	d
a	p	i	e	r	a
c	a	i	a	a	r
e	p	f	m	p	k
a	e	c	o	i	n
t	r	a	i	n	s

2. Now, find the mystery answer. Color it **purple** and write it on the line below.

What has hands but no feet?

1. Find and color these words **green**.

hands	**time**	**feet**	**sleep**
ring	**bug**	**bells**	

<table>
<tr><td>b</td><td>e</td><td>l</td><td>l</td><td>s</td><td>t</td></tr>
<tr><td>s</td><td>a</td><td>b</td><td>u</td><td>g</td><td>i</td></tr>
<tr><td>l</td><td>r</td><td>i</td><td>n</td><td>g</td><td>m</td></tr>
<tr><td>e</td><td>f</td><td>e</td><td>e</td><td>t</td><td>e</td></tr>
<tr><td>e</td><td>c</td><td>l</td><td>o</td><td>c</td><td>k</td></tr>
<tr><td>p</td><td>h</td><td>a</td><td>n</td><td>d</td><td>s</td></tr>
</table>

2. Now, find the mystery answer. Color it **yellow** and write it on the line below.

____

Name ______________________________ Word Search

Numbers

M	A	Z	T	S	I	X
T	E	N	W	X	O	P
Y	I	F	O	U	R	O
F	G	S	E	V	E	N
I	H	L	N	I	N	E
V	T	H	R	E	E	B
E	C	D	E	F	G	H

ONE
TWO
THREE

FOUR
FIVE
SIX
SEVEN

EIGHT
NINE
TEN

Brainwork! How old are you? ______

Write the number word. ______________________________

Name ______________________________ Word Search

Colors

A	Y	E	L	L	O	W
B	R	O	W	N	R	E
R	B	B	H	O	A	B
E	E	L	I	C	N	L
D	A	U	T	U	G	A
G	R	E	E	N	E	C
P	U	R	P	L	E	K

Extra Word! What animal is brown? ___ ___ ___ ___

Name ______________________________ Word Search

Farm Animals

J	S	H	E	E	P	E
U	B	F	Q	C	O	W
G	O	A	T	H	N	A
H	O	R	S	E	Y	L
O	K	M	O	N	E	L
G	H	E	C	A	L	F
M	I	R	B	U	L	L

COW	HOG	HORSE
CALF	SHEEP	HEN
PONY	BULL	GOAT

Extra Word! Who takes care of the farm animals?

___ ___ ___ ___ ___ ___ ___

Name ______________________________ Word Search

Body Parts

F	O	O	T	L	B	A
N	J	H	E	A	D	L
V	P	A	Z	M	O	L
B	K	N	O	S	E	E
E	X	D	U	F	Y	G
A	R	M	W	H	E	P
R	C	E	S	K	I	N

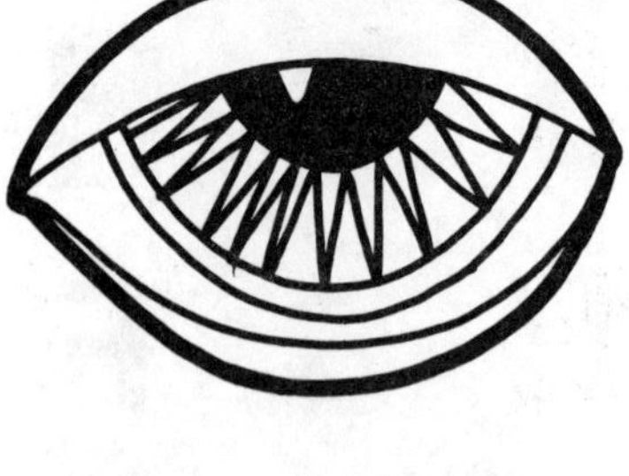

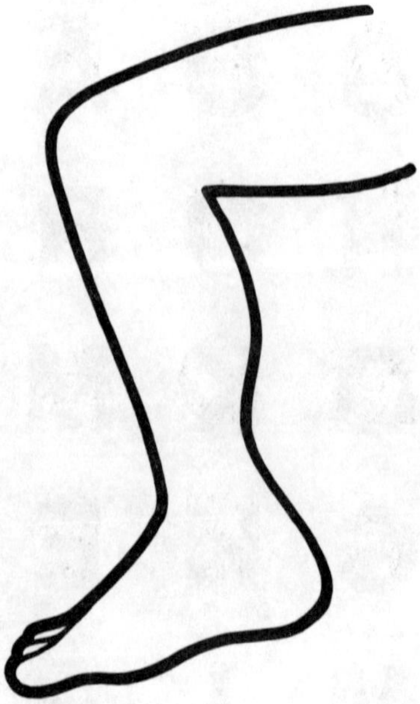

HAND	ARM	EAR
FOOT	LEG	NOSE
HEAD	EYE	SKIN

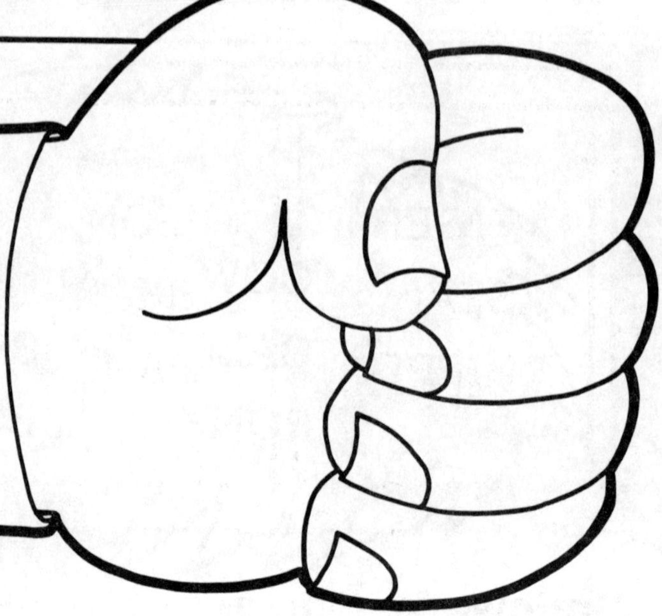

Brainwork! What word is a kind of ball? __ __ __ __ ball

Name ______________________________ Word Search

Zoo Animals

S	H	T	B	E	A	R
E	I	W	X	T	L	B
A	P	E	L	I	O	N
L	P	A	T	G	F	N
M	O	N	K	E	Y	V
A	Z	E	B	R	A	H
Y	I	P	A	N	D	A

TIGER	LION	MONKEY
SEAL	BEAR	ZEBRA
HIPPO	PANDA	APE

Brainwork! Find two animals with stripes.

_ _ _ _ _ , _ _ _ _ _ _ _ _

Name ______________________________ Word Search

Clothing

Z	A	S	H	O	E	L
F	S	K	D	H	A	T
S	H	I	R	T	X	M
O	O	R	E	L	C	R
C	R	T	S	W	O	K
K	T	Y	S	N	A	P
E	S	P	A	N	T	S

Brainwork! Find two words that rhyme.

_ _ _ _ _ , _ _ _ _ _ _

Name ______________________________ Word Search

Things That Go

T	R	U	C	K	P	L
B	O	A	T	J	O	M
I	C	E	R	C	A	R
K	K	X	A	B	N	B
J	E	T	I	U	C	I
D	T	F	N	S	G	K
T	R	P	L	A	N	E

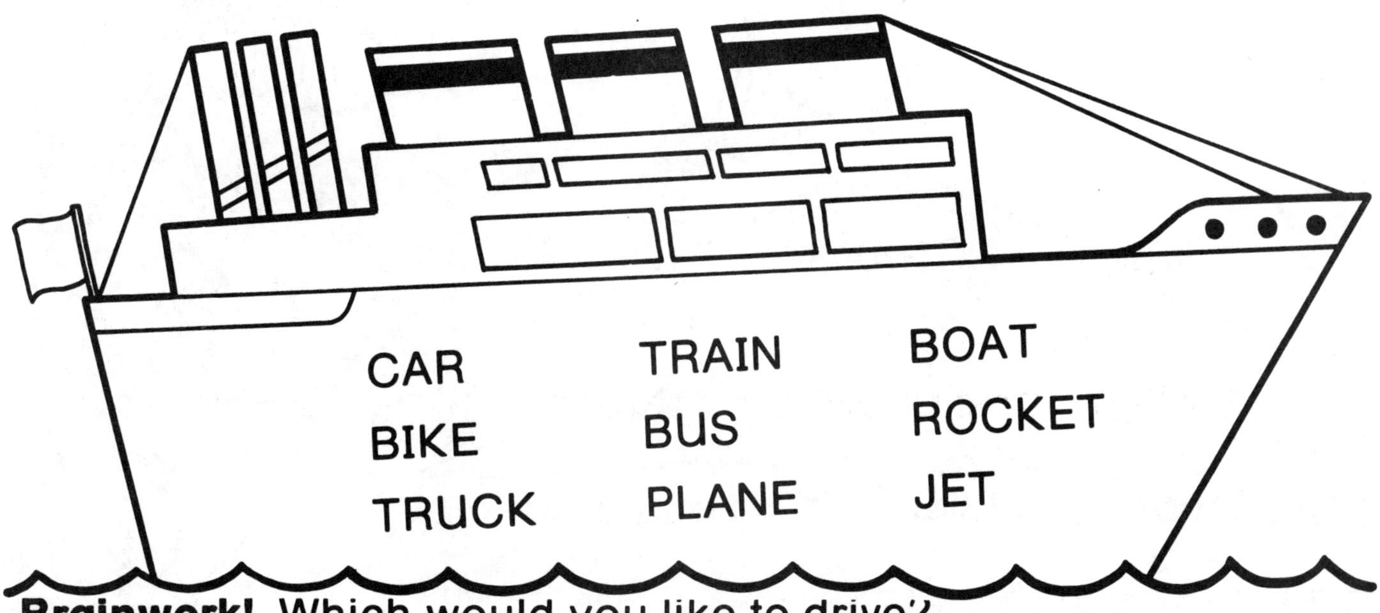

CAR TRAIN BOAT

BIKE BUS ROCKET

TRUCK PLANE JET

Brainwork! Which would you like to drive? ______________

Name ______________________________ Word Search

Outdoors

O	B	R	O	C	K	G
L	I	T	T	E	R	R
P	R	A	R	K	H	A
A	D	D	E	N	I	S
T	C	R	E	E	K	S
H	F	L	O	W	E	R
A	N	I	M	A	L	T

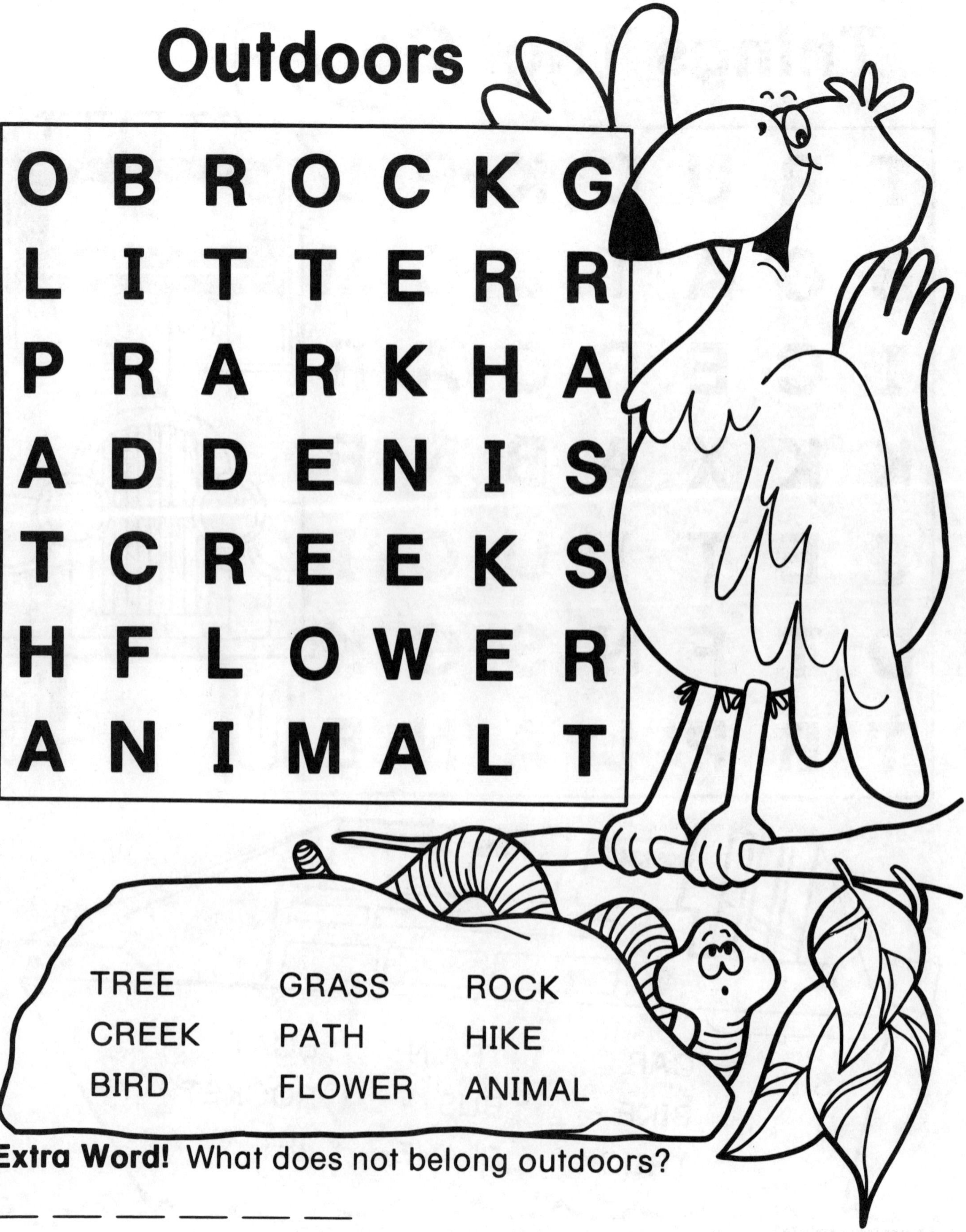

TREE	GRASS	ROCK
CREEK	PATH	HIKE
BIRD	FLOWER	ANIMAL

Extra Word! What does not belong outdoors?

___ ___ ___ ___ ___ ___

Name ______________________________ Word Search

Feelings

S	I	L	L	Y	S	G
T	E	L	L	G	A	R
H	I	B	O	L	D	I
A	C	O	W	A	E	N
P	R	O	U	D	N	S
P	O	H	U	R	T	H
Y	P	E	N	J	O	Y

HAPPY
SAD HURT
JOY PROUD BOLD
SILLY GLAD SHY

Extra Word! When I feel happy, I __ __ __ __ __

Name ______________________ Word Search

Birds

M	D	U	C	K	B	K
D	O	T	S	G	U	R
C	V	J	O	U	G	O
R	E	A	G	L	E	B
O	A	Y	E	L	L	I
W	T	T	W	R	E	N
P	P	A	R	R	O	T

Extra Word! What rhymes with hug? __ __ __

Name ______________________________ Word Search

Pets

T	B	I	R	D	G	O
H	E	N	A	D	O	G
E	G	G	T	I	R	E
H	A	M	S	T	E	R
Y	F	I	S	H	A	B
E	P	C	A	T	T	I
S	E	E	B	I	L	L

DOG	HAMSTER
CAT	GERBIL
BIRD	FISH
RATS	MICE

Extra Word! A bird eats with a _ _ _ _ .

Name ______________________ Word Search

Weather

P S F H A I L

C L O U D Y M

B E G S N O W

O E U R S R T

O T O A U N O

T B W I N D Y

S O W N Y E T

SNOW
RAIN
HAIL
CLOUDY
SLEET
SUN
FOG
WINDY

Extra Word! What do you wear on a rainy day?

__ __ __ __ __

Name ____________________

Sports Action

J	R	U	N	K	I	C
U	I	S	W	I	M	X
M	D	K	A	C	K	R
G	E	A	J	K	G	I
R	U	T	J	U	M	P
U	M	E	Z	J	O	G
H	O	P	S	W	I	N

RUN
HOP

KICK
JUMP

SKATE
SWIM

RIDE
JOG

Brainwork! Which do you like to do best? ____________

Name ______________________________ Word Search

Food

D	O	C	P	L	U	M
S	T	A	M	I	L	K
A	B	R	E	A	D	S
P	O	R	A	M	P	T
P	A	O	T	O	E	O
L	T	T	N	Y	A	V
E	C	H	E	E	S	E

CHEESE APPLE BREAD
MILK PEAS CARROT
MEAT PLUM

Extra Word! What can help you cook? __ __ __ __ __ __

Name ______________________________ Word Search

Insects

F	W	Z	T	M	P	I
L	A	D	Y	B	U	G
E	S	N	T	E	O	X
A	P	B	E	E	L	A
F	O	M	O	T	H	N
M	M	P	F	L	Y	T
D	H	O	N	E	Y	R

BEE
MOTH
FLY
WASP
FLEA
LADYBUG
ANT
BEETLE

Extra Word! Something sticky is __ __ __ __ __

Name ______________________________ Word Search

Seashore

F	I	S	H	T	B	G
N	O	P	M	L	A	U
R	W	S	H	E	L	L
P	A	I	L	R	L	L
L	T	F	S	A	N	D
T	E	S	H	I	P	X
C	R	A	B	O	A	T

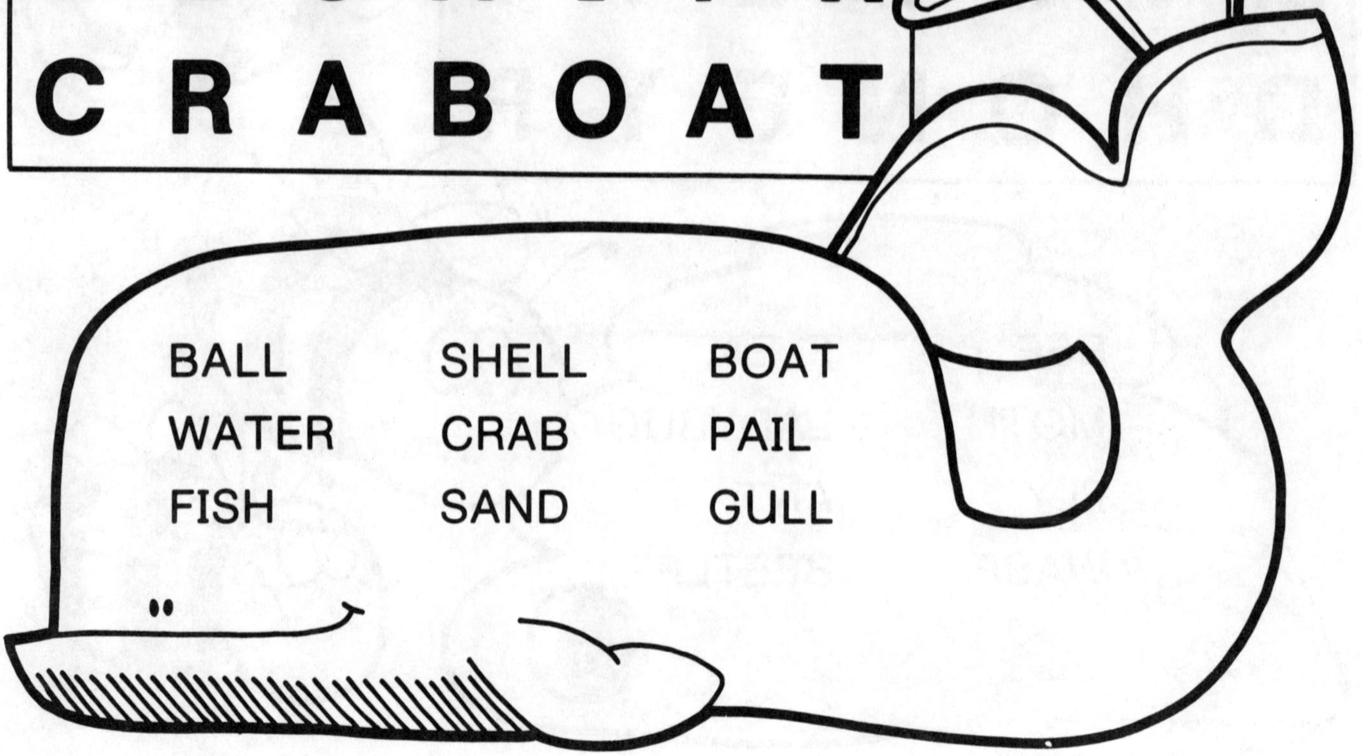

BALL	SHELL	BOAT
WATER	CRAB	PAIL
FISH	SAND	GULL

Extra Word! What is bigger than a boat? __ __ __ __

Name ______________________

Schoolroom

B	N	K	R	A	C	T
N	U	X	U	T	H	A
F	L	A	G	M	A	B
B	P	E	N	C	I	L
O	R	D	O	O	R	E
O	L	M	D	E	S	K
K	W	I	N	D	O	W

PENCIL DESK FLAG
CHAIR TABLE WINDOW
BOOK DOOR RUG

Brainwork! A __ __ __ __ is red, white and blue.

Name ______________________________ Word Search

Workers

W	P	E	R	T	W	D
F	A	R	M	E	R	E
T	I	C	P	A	I	N
E	N	L	I	C	T	T
A	T	E	L	H	E	I
C	E	R	O	E	R	S
N	R	K	T	R	E	T

PAINTER FARMER WRITER
TEACHER DENTIST PILOT
CLERK

Brainwork! Which worker would you like to watch?

____

Name ______________________________

Science

W	D	M	O	O	N	C
O	R	B	I	T	I	B
S	E	E	K	N	S	L
P	L	A	N	E	T	U
A	S	R	V	X	A	E
C	U	T	O	T	R	T
E	N	H	A	S	K	Y

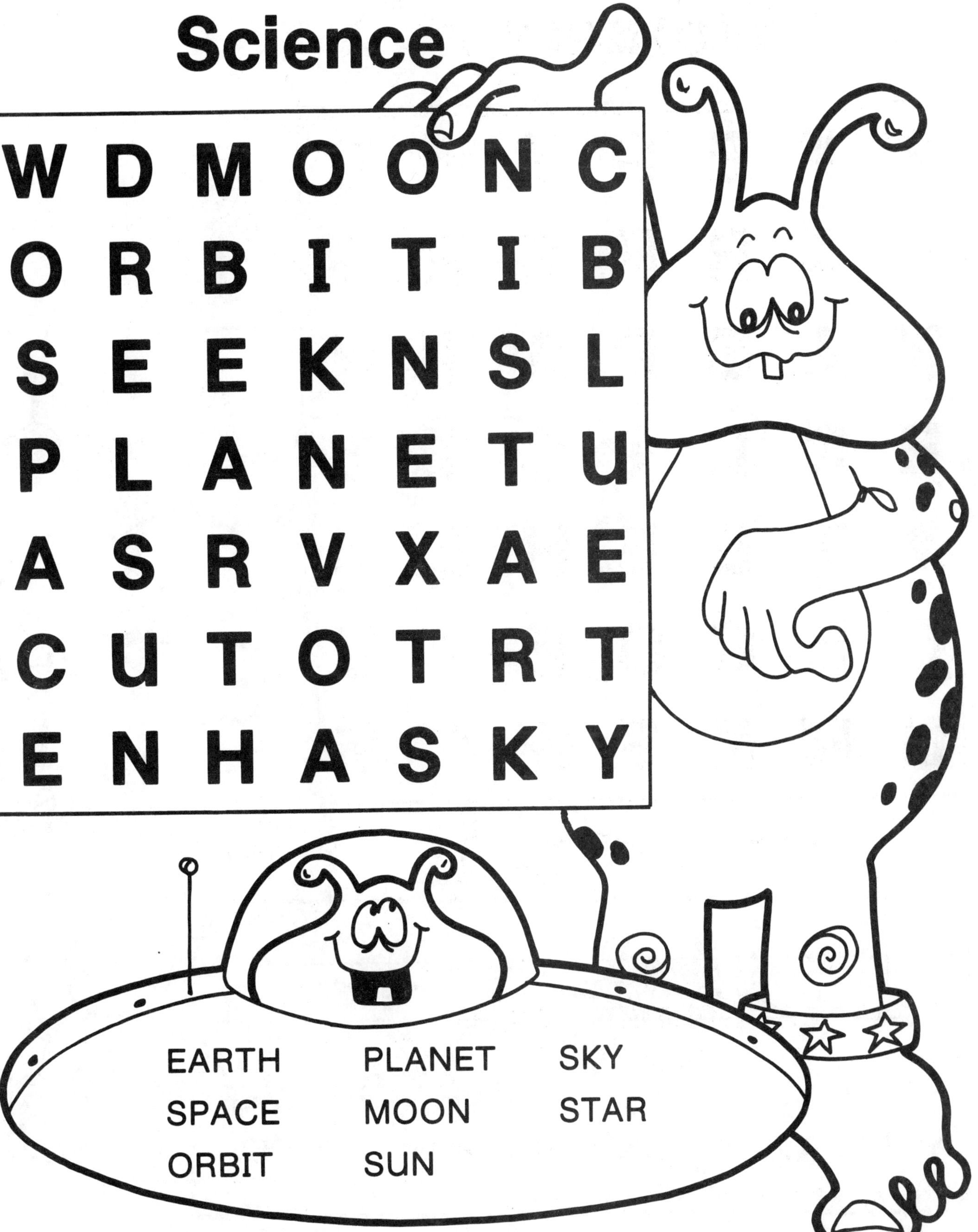

EARTH	PLANET	SKY
SPACE	MOON	STAR
ORBIT	SUN	

Extra Word! What color is the sky? __ __ __ __ __

Name ______________________________ Word Search

Tools

F	X	D	O	Z	H	P
U	T	R	P	S	A	W
N	A	I	L	S	M	R
R	C	L	I	C	M	E
Y	K	L	E	R	E	N
P	S	C	R	E	R	C
D	M	N	S	W	P	H

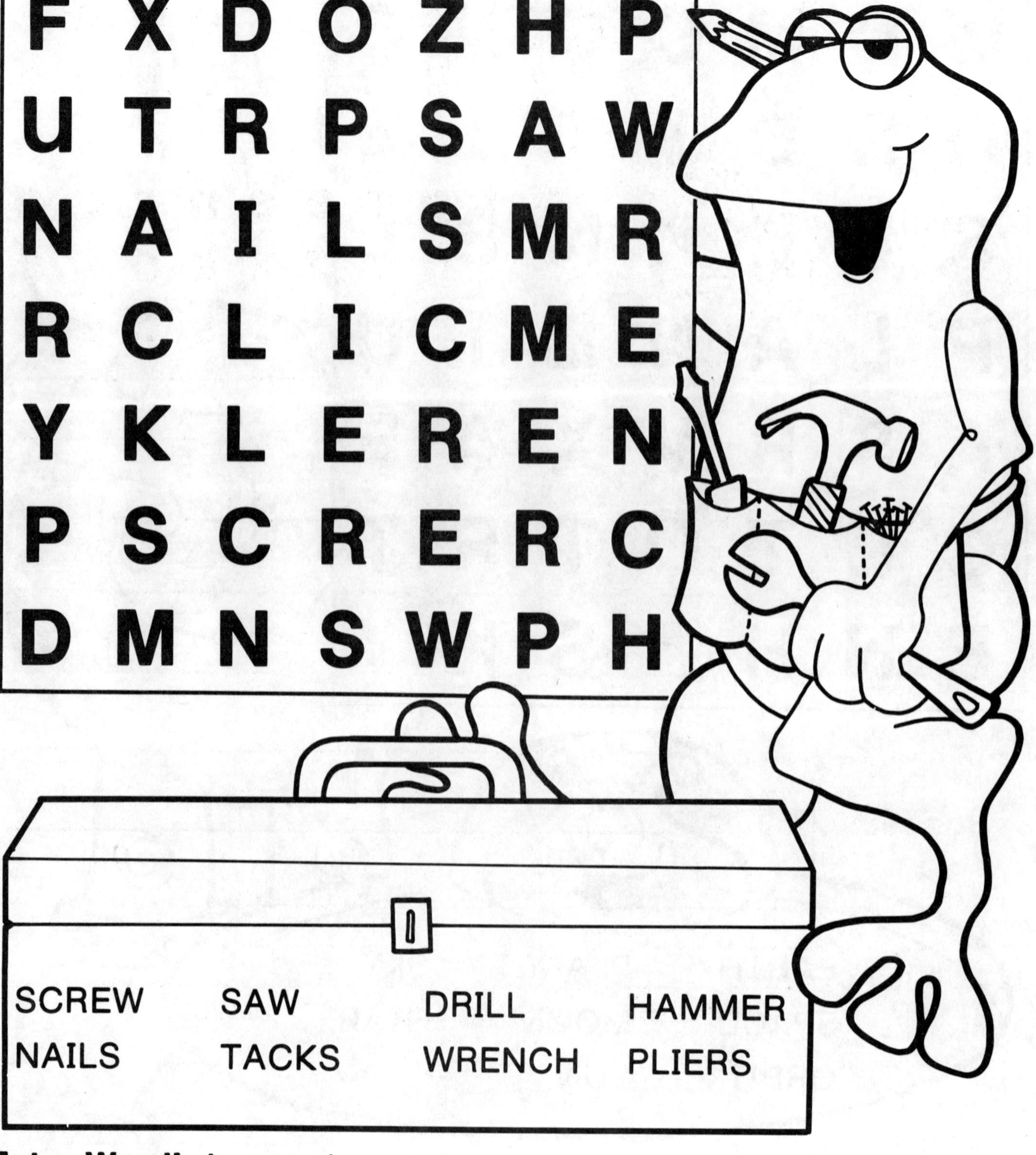

SCREW SAW DRILL HAMMER
NAILS TACKS WRENCH PLIERS

Extra Word! A party is ___ ___ ___.

Name ______________________ Skill: Sight word comprehension, Word search

The Little Frog

afraid
green
frog
take
little
real
park
school

l	g	a	f	r	a	i	d	s
i	p	a	r	k	o	a	z	c
t	c	q	r	n	t	f	t	h
t	g	r	e	e	n	r	a	o
l	h	v	a	x	k	o	k	o
e	p	m	l	l	s	g	e	l

1. Jan has a little green ______________________.
   frog   for   from

2. The little frog is ______________________.
   rest   read   real

3. Jan found it in the ______________________.
   pan   park   pat

4. Jan is not ______________________.
   after   afraid   away

5. She will take the frog to ______________________.
   school   real   green

Name ______________________

Skill: Sight word comprehension, Word search

The Shaggy Dog

big
dog
ran
park
rest
shaggy
tree
after

r	a	n	b	k	d	o	s
s	h	x	i	v	m	q	h
d	l	n	g	u	z	r	a
o	a	f	t	e	r	e	g
g	t	r	e	e	f	s	g
w	p	a	r	k	y	t	y

1. The shaggy dog was ______________ and white.
   big dog bug

2. The big dog ran in the ______________.
   park play pan

3. The dog ran ______________ the squirrels.
   away and after

4. The squirrels ran up the ______________.
   the tree three

5. The dog sat down to ______________.
   rest red real

Name ____________________ Skill: Sight word comprehension, Word search

The Little Kitten

- little
- cute
- keep
- kittens
- six
- name
- soft
- white

s	o	f	t	c	u	t	e
l	i	t	t	l	e	v	t
e	x	a	w	k	z	d	n
k	i	t	t	e	n	s	a
w	h	i	t	e	b	i	m
m	u	c	f	p	k	x	e

1. Pat's cat had six ____________________.
   kittens kite keep

2. Pat likes the ____________________ white one.
   like little look

3. The little kitten is ____________________ and soft.
   can cut cute

4. Pat will ____________________ the white kitten.
   kite keep kitten

5. She will ____________________ it Snowball.
   name man not

Name ________________________ Skill: Sight word comprehension, Word search

Good Friends

f	r	i	e	n	d	s	c
p	x	t	s	i	t	s	a
o	h	u	n	g	r	y	r
l	i	t	t	l	e	b	r
s	e	i	c	t	a	u	o
r	a	b	b	i	t	g	t

1. The rabbit has a good ________________.
   clean carrot came

2. It is a ________________ rabbit.
   hopped have hungry

3. A little red bug ________________ on the street.
   said sits sad

4. The bug and rabbit are ________________.
   find flower friends

5. They will ________________ the carrot.
   eat eye eel

Name ______________________ Skill: Sight word comprehension, Word search

Baby Frogs

found
frogs
pond
jar
tadpoles
them
watch
grow

b	p	f	t	h	e	m	f
j	o	o	g	r	o	w	r
a	n	u	d	v	k	y	o
r	d	n	x	g	z	q	g
t	a	d	p	o	l	e	s
h	w	a	t	c	h	o	u

1. Kim went to the ______________________.
   pan   pond   found

2. She found some ______________________.
   tadpoles   the   found

3. Kim put them in a ______________________.
   jump   jar   far

4. She will watch them ______________________.
   grow   frogs   green

5. They will grow into ______________________.
   found   far   frogs

Name ______________________________

Skill: Sight word comprehension, Word search

Something Good

- cake
- come
- hole
- eat
- cat
- little
- mouse
- smell

e	a	t	l	c	o	m	e
r	h	p	i	h	z	o	u
c	k	b	t	o	x	u	c
a	f	x	t	l	v	s	a
t	m	q	l	e	c	e	k
g	s	m	e	l	l	j	e

1. The mouse can ______________ something good.
   smell small came

2. The mouse is out of its ______________.
   have hole had

3. The mouse sees a little bit of ______________.
   cat cake came

4. It does not see the ______________.
   cat cake came

5. The mouse will ______________ the cake.
   cat came eat

Name ______________________ Skill: Sight word comprehension, Word search

Tim's Bird

bird
hand
cage
blue
hi
little
say
sit

m	l	y	b	u	h	c	k
s	i	t	i	c	a	g	e
r	t	o	r	v	n	w	s
s	t	j	d	z	d	v	f
a	l	q	x	b	l	u	e
y	e	g	p	x	h	i	b

1. Tim has a pet ______________________.
   blue bird band

2. The bird is little and ______________________.
   blue bird band

3. The bird can sit on his ______________________.
   hello had hand

4. Tim's bird can ______________________, "Hi!"
   sat say sit

5. The bird lives in a ______________________.
   cage came cake

Name ______________________

Skill: Sight word comprehension, Word search

My Funny Pet

eat
farm
fat
pig
food
mud
funny
roll

b	f	u	n	n	y	g	r
f	s	k	p	t	f	v	o
o	j	c	i	h	a	e	l
o	w	p	g	o	t	a	l
d	f	a	r	m	x	t	k
y	d	q	m	u	d	z	m

1. My pig is big and ______________________.
   farm fat fun

2. My pig is on a ______________________.
   farm fun fat

3. It likes to ______________________ food.
   fat eat mud

4. It likes to ______________________ in the mud.
   roll rat for

5. I love my ______________________ pet.
   food run funny

Name ______________________ Skill: Sight word comprehension, Word search

A Surprise

big
all
birthday
door
friends
party
great
surprise

b	i	r	t	h	d	a	y
p	a	r	t	y	o	b	x
f	z	a	l	l	o	i	h
g	r	e	a	t	r	g	k
f	r	i	e	n	d	s	n
s	u	r	p	r	i	s	e

1. Pam peeked around the ______________.
   door do doing

2. She saw a big ______________.
   some surprise say

3. It was a birthday ______________.
   party pan pat

4. All of her ______________ were there.
   find four friends

5. It was a ______________ party.
   great green doing

Name ______________________

Skill: Sight word comprehension,
Word search

A Duck Family

k	b	r	o	w	n	y	g
q	y	m	o	t	h	e	r
b	p	c	j	w	b	l	x
a	o	s	w	i	m	l	b
b	n	v	d	z	f	o	i
y	d	u	c	k	s	w	g

1. Two ducks are in the ________________.
   pond   brown   down

2. Mother duck is big and ________________.
   brown   down   duck

3. A little duck is ________________.
   yellow   yes   swim

4. The ducks like to ________________ and splash.
   swim   star   sky

5. The baby duck will swim with its ________________.
   moon   mother   many

Name ____________________

Skill: Sight word comprehension, Word search

Fun at the Park

ball
after
bat
friends
game
fun
park
school

b	a	t	f	p	f	u	n
a	f	r	i	e	n	d	s
l	t	d	z	q	e	y	g
l	e	v	p	a	r	k	a
j	r	s	m	x	b	r	m
s	c	h	o	o	l	k	e

1. After school, Joe went to the ____________________.
   park after pat

2. He took his ____________________ and ball.
   bit bat bet

3. He met his ____________________ in the park.
   find friends after

4. They played a ____________________.
   game park good

5. They had ____________________ in the park.
   bat after fun

Name ______________________________ Skill: Sight word comprehension, Word search

Bozo Bear

ball
bear
spin
circus
live
dance
people
tricks

d	a	n	c	e	a	j	p
f	c	i	r	c	u	s	e
b	s	p	i	n	d	k	o
e	g	r	l	i	v	e	p
a	l	c	w	b	a	l	l
r	t	r	i	c	k	s	e

1. Bozo Bear lives in a ______________________.
   circus clap cat

2. He can do many ______________________.
   tricks roll this

3. Bozo Bear can spin and ______________________.
   don't bear dance

4. He can roll on a big ______________________.
   ball roll band

5. ______________________ like to see Bozo.
   Roll People Dance

Name ______________________

Skill: Sight word comprehension, Word search

Trip to the Moon

rocks
far
man
fly
moon
rocket
up
walk

m	a	n	c	g	w	f	n
r	g	f	a	r	a	l	y
o	z	u	v	q	l	y	m
c	c	p	k	x	k	v	o
k	r	o	c	k	e	t	o
s	j	l	e	m	a	r	n

1. The man will go in the ______________________.
   rich rocket rock

2. The rocket will ______________________ to the moon.
   fly far fish

3. The moon is ______________________ away.
   farm fast far

4. The man will ______________________ on the moon.
   was want walk

5. He will look at the ______________________.
   rocks far ran

Name ______________________

Skill: Sight word comprehension, Word search

A New Toy

balloon
bear
brown
hug
little
soft
toy

s	o	f	t	b	r	z	l
v	d	s	m	r	b	f	i
b	a	l	l	o	o	n	t
e	k	h	o	w	q	x	t
a	c	u	v	n	y	g	l
r	j	g	e	t	o	y	e

1. I have a new ______________.
   toy the to

2. It is a little brown ______________.
   beg bear best

3. I love to give it a ______________.
   have had hug

4. It is ______________ and brown.
   so saw soft

5. My bear has a little ______________.
   bring balloon big

Name ______________________________

Skill: Sight word comprehension, Word search

Visit to the Doctor

arm
doctor
fell
hurt
play
running
street
fix

h	f	e	l	l	e	k	s
q	i	x	y	h	u	r	t
y	x	d	o	c	t	o	r
a	i	p	l	a	y	d	e
r	u	n	n	i	n	g	e
m	z	b	u	j	z	s	t

1. Ted was running down the ______________________________.
   hurt   street   said

2. He fell and hurt his ______________________________.
   am   arm   at

3. Ted went to see a ______________________________.
   doctor   don't   doing

4. The doctor will ______________________________ Ted's arm.
   fox   fell   fix

5. Ted cannot ______________________________ a game.
   play   played   playing

Name ______________________ Skill: Sight word comprehension, Word search

Sammy Seal

bark
circus
seal
horn
play
have
clap
trick

c	i	b	q	h	o	r	n
i	h	a	v	e	y	s	t
r	d	r	c	s	w	e	r
c	j	k	l	p	c	a	i
u	a	z	a	f	s	l	c
s	k	m	p	l	a	y	k

1. Come to see the ______________________.
   clap circus come

2. You will see Sammy the ______________________.
   see sees seal

3. Sammy will do a ______________________ for you.
   truck trick this

4. Sammy can play the ______________________.
   horn have had

5. Sammy can clap and ______________________.
   bark big bad

Name ____________________ Skill: Sight word comprehension, Word search

A Letter for Fran

away
every
for
letter
hear
lives
week
from

w	e	e	k	l	e	g	f
o	s	l	e	t	t	e	r
y	f	o	r	d	u	a	o
e	v	e	r	y	p	w	m
z	l	i	v	e	s	a	e
h	e	a	r	k	z	y	s

1. Fran got a ____________________ today.
   let little letter

2. The letter was ____________________ her grandmother.
   four from far

3. Fran likes to ____________________ from her grandmother.
   her hear had

4. Her grandmother lives far ____________________.
   away every and

5. Her grandmother writes every ____________________.
   walk we week

Name ______________________________

Skill: Sight word comprehension,
Word search

Hide-and-Seek

a	w	a	y	g	t	r	g
f	y	t	u	r	t	l	e
t	j	a	d	a	f	o	t
e	r	e	o	s	i	i	z
r	c	x	g	s	n	i	g
p	o	n	d	k	d	s	y

1. A turtle came out of the ______________________.
   pond hid dog

2. The turtle hid in the ______________________.
   good grass dog

3. A big dog came to ______________________ it.
   find bad hid

4. The dog did not ______________________ the turtle.
   good dog get

5. The dog went ______________________.
   after away and

Name ______________________

Skill: Sight word comprehension, Word search

Bobo

circus
clap
face
funny
laugh
tricks
like

l	f	a	c	e	c	c	t
i	l	v	i	q	l	l	r
k	a	e	r	k	o	a	i
e	u	g	c	t	w	p	c
x	g	f	u	n	n	y	k
w	h	m	s	j	z	m	s

1. Bobo is a funny ______________________.
   clown clap circus

2. He works in a ______________________.
   clown clap circus

3. He likes to make people ______________________.
   laugh like little

4. He does funny ______________________.
   trucks tricks funny

5. He has a funny ______________________.
   fat face funny

Name ________________________________

Skill: Sight word comprehension, Word search

The Little Bee

cat
good
little
grass
looked
up
sky
went

k	g	r	a	s	s	f	l
l	o	o	k	e	d	e	i
r	o	m	x	j	c	y	t
b	d	u	p	t	a	d	t
w	e	n	t	w	t	m	l
s	u	l	s	k	y	v	e

1. The cat sat down in the ________________.
   good grass get

2. The cat ________________ at the bee.
   little liked looked

3. The little bee ________________ up.
   will went where

4. The bee went up and ________________.
   up sun to

5. The bee went up in the ________________.
   something said sky

Answer Key

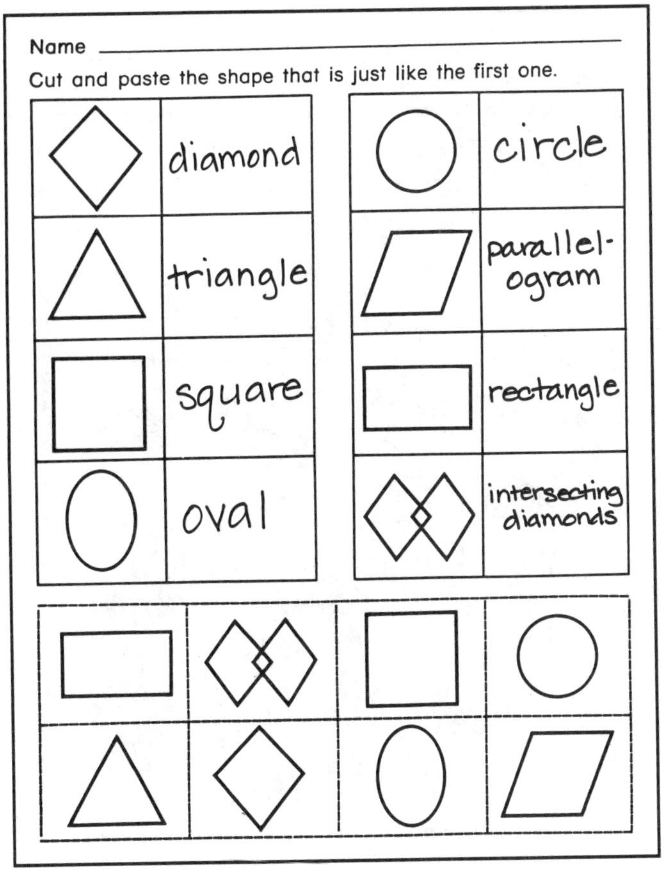
Name ______________________

Cut and paste the shape that is just like the first one.

Page 1

Name ______________________

Look at the picture. With a brown crayon, color all the animals that are alike. Color the rest of the picture in your favorite colors.

Page 2

Name ______________________

Mrs. Bunny has lots of children. It's hard to tell them apart. Color the bunnies that are different.

Page 3

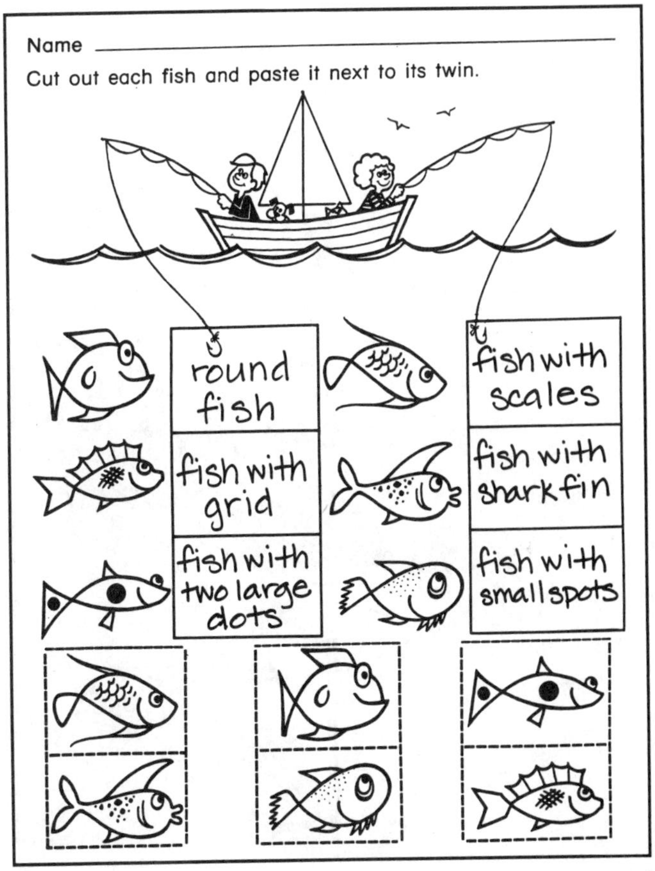
Name ______________________

Cut out each fish and paste it next to its twin.

Page 4

Answer Key

Name ______________________________

The bears in the forest are having a party. Color the bears that are different.

Page 5

Name ______________________________

Look at Farmer Fred's hens. Color the hens that are alike.

Page 6

Name ______________________________

Look at the road. Color the cars that are alike.

Page 7

Name ______________________________

Cut out the boats below. Paste them in the right places.

Page 8

Answer Key

Name ____________
It's a windy day! Color all the kites that are different.

Page 9

Name ____________
Cut and paste each twin.

Page 10

Name ____________
Cut and paste each face next to its twin.

Page 11

Name ____________
Color the flowers that are different.

Page 12

Answer Key

Name ______________________________

It's a snowy day. Circle all the snowflakes that are alike. Color the picture.

Page 13

Name ______________________________

Color the cards that are alike in each row.

Page 14

Name ______________________________

Cut and paste the pictures that are alike.

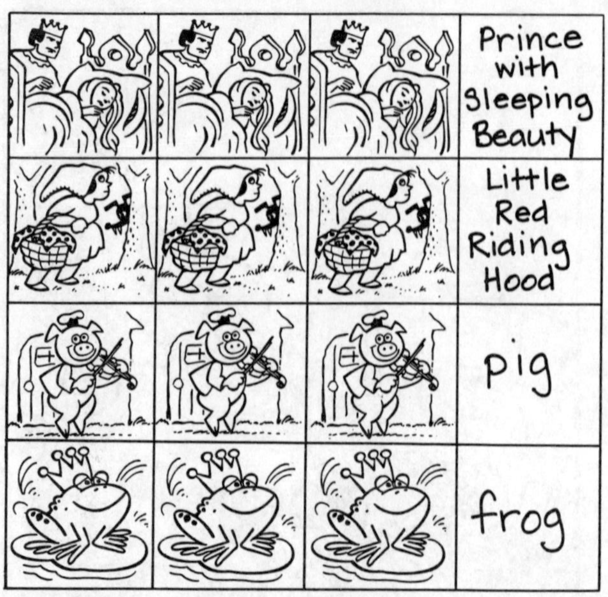

Page 15

Name ______________________________

Look at each row. Color the pictures that are different from the first one.

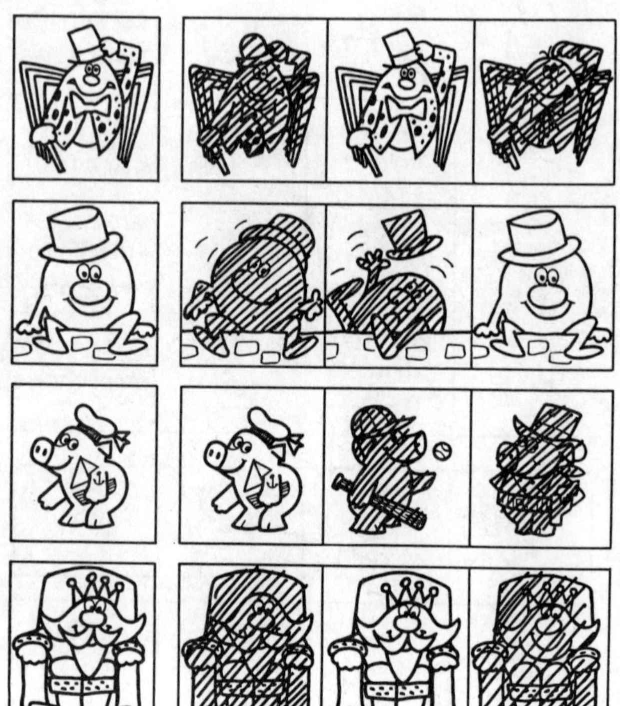

Page 16

Answer Key

Name ______________________

Ann wants to give her friend a set of her vacation pictures. Cut and paste each picture next to the one that is alike.

Page 17

Name ______________________

Color the vegetables and trees that are alike.

Page 18

Name ______________________

It's raining cats and dogs! Color all the cats, dogs and umbrellas that are alike.

Page 19

Name ______________________

Color everything that is alike in each row.

Page 20

Answer Key

Name ______________________________ Skill: Visual perception—short vowel a words

Word Box

apple	cat	fan	hat
map	bat	glass	tack
clam	flag	candle	lamb

Find the pictures of the words from the Word Box. Color them.

Page 21

Name ______________________________ Skill: Visual perception—short vowel e words

Word Box

bed	dress	hen	net
bell	egg	jet	pen
desk	fence	nest	web

Find the pictures of the words from the Word Box. Color them.

Page 22

Name ______________________________ Skill: Visual perception—short vowel i words

Word Box

chick	king	pig	whistle
fish	milk	pin	wig
hill	mitt	ship	zipper

Find the pictures of the words from the Word Box. Color them.

Page 23

Name ______________________________ Skill: Visual perception—short vowel u words

Word Box

bug	duck	hut	rug
bus	bun	nut	sun
cup	jug	umbrella	truck

Find the pictures of the words from the Word Box. Color them.

Page 24

Answer Key

Name ____________________ Skill: Visual perception—long vowel i words

Word Box

~~bride~~	~~five~~	~~tire~~	~~nine~~
~~file~~	~~ice~~	~~vine~~	~~prize~~
~~fire~~	~~kite~~	~~mice~~	~~wire~~

Find the pictures of the words from the Word Box. Color them.

Page 25

Name ____________________ Skill: Visual perception—numbers 11-20

Find the numerals from 11-20. Color them orange.
Color the rest of the picture.

Page 26

Name ____________________ Skill: Visual perception—rhyming words

Word Box

~~man~~	~~hat~~	~~pop~~	~~pet~~
~~fan~~	~~cat~~	~~mop~~	~~net~~
~~pan~~	~~mat~~	~~top~~	~~jet~~

Find the pictures of the words from the Word Box. Color them.

Page 27

Name ____________________ Skill: Visual perception—farm animals

Word Box

~~pig~~	~~horse~~	~~rabbit~~	~~goose~~
~~hen~~	~~dog~~	~~sheep~~	~~goat~~
~~cow~~	~~cat~~	~~duck~~	~~turkey~~

Find the pictures of the words from the Word Box. Color them.

Page 28

Answer Key

Name ____________________ Skill: Visual perception—compound words

Word Box

~~baseball~~ ~~doghouse~~ ~~popcorn~~ ~~spaceship~~
~~beehive~~ ~~football~~ ~~sailboat~~ ~~starfish~~
~~butterfly~~ ~~paintbrush~~ ~~schoolhouse~~ ~~sunflower~~

Find the pictures of the words from the Word Box. Color them.

Page 29

Name ____________________ Skill: Visual perception — compound words

Word Box

~~basketball~~ ~~clothespin~~ ~~overalls~~ ~~rainbow~~
~~bulldog~~ ~~handcuff~~ ~~pancakes~~ ~~watermelon~~
~~clipboard~~ ~~haystack~~ ~~peanuts~~ ~~windmill~~

Find the pictures of the words from the Word Box. Color them.

Page 30

Name ____________________ Skill: Visual perception—consonant blends

Word Box

~~swing~~ ~~slide~~ ~~skunk~~ ~~spoon~~
~~sled~~ ~~swan~~ ~~spider~~ ~~skis~~
~~sweater~~ ~~sleeping bag~~ ~~skate~~ ~~space suit~~

Find the pictures of the words from the Word Box. Color them.

Page 31

Name ____________________ Skill: Completing sentences, Following directions

Read the sentences to find out how to color the picture.

bird rabbit sand sun

1. The yellow sun was in the sky.
2. The rabbit has a green pail.
3. The brown rabbit sat in the sand.
4. A blue bird was on the log.
5. The brown log was in the sand.
6. A red crab was in the yellow sand.

Page 32

Answer Key

Name ______________________ Skill: Completing sentences, Following directions

Read the sentences to find out how to color the picture.

box dog grass wagon

1. An orange hat was on the **dog**.
2. The brown dog was on the **grass**.
3. Three yellow eggs are in a **wagon**.
4. The red wagon is on the **grass**.
5. A brown hen sat in the **box**.
6. The black box is on the green **grass**.

Page 33

Name ______________________ Skill: Completing sentences, Following directions

Read the sentences to find out how to color the picture.

grass hat turtle mouse

1. A black **hat** was on the rabbit.
2. The brown rabbit was on the **grass**.
3. A black **mouse** sat on the turtle.
4. A red hat was on the green **turtle**.
5. The turtle was on the green **grass**.
6. A red bug was on the **grass**.

Page 34

Name ______________________ Skill: Completing sentences, Following directions

Read the sentences to find out how to color the picture.

box cat dog grass

1. The **cat** has a red kite.
2. The orange **cat** sat in a chair.
3. The blue chair was on the **grass**.
4. A black **dog** sat in the box.
5. The yellow box was on the green **grass**.
6. A brown mouse was on the **grass**.

Page 35

Name ______________________ Skill: Completing sentences, Following directions

Read the sentences to find out how to color the picture.

balloon book box grass

1. The mouse has a red **balloon**.
2. The brown mouse sat on a **box**.
3. The blue box was on the **grass**.
4. The orange cat sat on the **grass**.
5. The dog has a yellow **book**.
6. The black dog sat on the green **grass**.

Page 36

Answer Key

Name ______________________ Skill: Completing sentences, Following directions

Read the sentences to find out how to color the picture.

box grass rabbit sun

1. The red hat was on the rabbit.
2. The brown rabbit was on the grass.
3. A big, black bear was on the grass.
4. A brown mouse sat on a box.
5. The blue box was on the green grass.
6. The yellow sun was in the sky.

Page 37

Name ______________________ Skill: Completing sentences, Following directions

Read the sentences to find out how to color the picture.

book box chair grass

1. The dog has a red book.
2. The black dog sat on a chair.
3. The blue chair was on the grass.
4. The orange bird was on the box.
5. The black box was on the green grass.
6. The brown snake was in the grass.

Page 38

Name ______________________ Skill: Completing sentences, Following directions

Read the sentences to find out how to color the picture.

bear bee box grass

1. The black rabbit hid in the grass.
2. A yellow duck sat in the box.
3. The orange box was on the grass.
4. A blue hat was on the brown bear.
5. The bear was on the green grass.
6. The yellow bee flew up and up.

Page 39

Name ______________________ Skill: Completing sentences, Following directions

Read the sentences to find out how to color the picture.

box fish grass jar

1. The red flag was in the box.
2. The orange cat was in the box.
3. The blue box was on the grass.
4. A red fish was in the jar.
5. A yellow duck looked into the jar.
6. The jar is on the green grass.

Page 40

Answer Key

Name ______________________ Skill: Completing sentences, Following directions

Read the sentences to find out how to color the picture.

bee box duck grass rabbit

1. The yellow bee flew.
2. The black mouse sat on a duck.
3. The yellow duck was on the grass.
4. A blue hat was on the rabbit.
5. The brown rabbit sat on a box.
6. The red box was on the green grass.

Page 41

Name ______________________ Skill: Completing sentences, Following directions

Read the sentences to find out how to color the picture.

box dog grass pig

1. The brown hen sat on the grass.
2. The blue star is on the pig.
3. The red pig sat in a box.
4. The yellow box is on the grass.
5. The red hat is on the black dog.
6. The dog was on the green grass.

Page 42

Name ______________________ Skill: Completing sentences, Following directions

Read the sentences to find out how to color the picture.

ball boat pond

1. The yellow duck sat in a boat.
2. The brown cat sat in a boat.
3. The boat was in the blue pond.
4. A red flag was on the green boat.
5. The seal has an orange ball.
6. The black seal swam in the pond.

Page 43

Name ______________________ Skill: Completing sentences, Following directions

Read the sentences to find out how to color the picture.

bear box dog mouse

1. The yellow hat was on a bear.
2. The brown bear was on a red ball.
3. The mouse has an orange balloon.
4. The black mouse sat on a dog.
5. The brown dog sat on a box.
6. Two red stars are on a blue box.

Page 44

Answer Key

Name ______________________ Skill: Completing sentences, Following directions

Read the sentences to find out how to color the picture.

bird cat rock sand

1. The red hat is on the cat.
2. The cat has a green pail.
3. The orange cat sat in the sand.
4. The bird has a red fish.
5. The black bird is on a brown rock.
6. The rock is in the yellow sand.

Page 45

Name ______________________ Skill: Completing sentences, Following directions

Read the sentences to find out how to color the picture.

box dog grass hat turtle

1. The red bug sat on the hat.
2. A blue hat was on the dog.
3. The brown dog got down from a box.
4. A black mouse sat on the turtle.
5. The green turtle was on the grass.
6. The yellow box was on the green grass.

Page 46

Name ______________________ Skill: Completing sentences, Following directions

Read the sentences to find out how to color the picture.

grass pond sun turtle

1. The yellow duck swam in the pond.
2. The red fish jumped in the blue pond.
3. The yellow sun was in the sky.
4. The red bug sat on the black turtle.
5. The turtle was on the green grass.
6. The brown dog was on the grass.

Page 47

Name ______________________ Skill: Completing sentences, Following directions

Read the sentences to find out how to color the picture.

ball can seal wagon

1. The brown dog hid in a can.
2. The black can is in a red wagon.
3. The yellow balloon is on the wagon.
4. A green hat is on the seal.
5. The black seal has a red ball.
6. The seal is on a blue box.

Page 48

Answer Key

Name ____________ Skill: Completing sentences. Following directions

Read the sentences to find out how to color the picture.

dog grass hat turtle

1. The green turtle was on the grass.
2. The black rabbit sat on the turtle.
3. A red bug sat on a blue hat.
4. A yellow duck was on the dog.
5. The brown dog was on the grass.
6. The dog was on the green grass.

Page 49

Name ____________ Skill: Completing sentences. Following directions

Read the sentences to find out how to color the picture.

cat grass hat

1. A black mouse sat in a blue hat.
2. The hat was on the green grass.
3. The yellow duck was on the grass.
4. The orange cat sat in the wagon.
5. The cat has a red balloon.
6. The red wagon was on the grass.

Page 50

Name ____________ Skill: Completing sentences. Following directions

Read the sentences to find out how to color the picture.

balloon bear bee box

1. The black cat has an orange balloon.
2. The cat sat in a blue box.
3. A blue hat is on a brown bear.
4. The bear has a red jar.
5. The bear sat in the green grass.
6. The yellow bee flew in the sky.

Page 51

What is the best paper to make kites from?

1. Find and color these words **yellow**.

~~chops~~ ~~cheer~~ ~~chimp~~

~~cheese~~ ~~chill~~ ~~it~~

c c h o p s
h c h e e r
e f l y i t
e c h i l l
s p a p e r
e c h i m p

2. Now, find the mystery answer. Color it **red** and write it on the line below.

fly paper

Page 52

Answer Key

What's the best thing to have?

1. Find and color these words **orange**.

~~horses~~ ~~drive~~ ~~fork~~ ~~soap~~
~~sleep~~ ~~smoke~~

f	s	l	e	e	p
o	d	r	i	v	e
r	a	s	o	a	p
k	s	m	o	k	e
f	r	i	e	n	d
h	o	r	s	e	s

2. Now, find the mystery answer. Color it **purple** and write it on the line below.

a friend

Page 53

What kind of dog has no tail?

1. Find and color these words **brown**.

~~cheese~~ ~~bun~~ ~~butter~~ ~~shop~~
~~man~~ ~~at~~ ~~he~~ ~~new~~

b	u	t	t	e	r
s	h	o	p	a	m
h	n	e	w	a	a
e	h	o	t	t	n
c	h	e	e	s	e
b	u	n	d	o	g

2. Now, find the mystery answer. Color it **yellow** and write it on the line below.

a hot dog

Page 54

What is a zebra after it is five years old?

1. Find and color these words **blue**.

~~feet~~ ~~dog~~ ~~up~~ ~~get~~
~~in~~ ~~color~~ ~~leg~~ ~~out~~

f	e	e	t	g	l
s	i	x	u	e	e
d	o	g	p	t	g
i	y	e	a	r	s
n	c	o	l	o	r
o	u	t	o	l	d

2. Now, find the mystery answer. Color it **yellow** and write it on the line below.

six years old

Page 55

What is red and eats rocks?

1. Find and color these words **yellow**.

~~duck~~ ~~I~~ ~~my~~ ~~day~~
~~sky~~ ~~blue~~ ~~slow~~ ~~do~~

s	a	b	l	u	e
k	d	r	e	d	s
y	o	d	a	y	l
r	o	c	k	m	o
d	u	c	k	y	w
l	e	a	t	e	r

2. Now, find the mystery answer. Color it **red** and write it on the line below.

a red rock eater

Page 56

Answer Key

What belongs only to you?

1. Find and color these words **yellow**.

~~shoes~~ ~~card~~ ~~not~~ ~~yes~~
~~hands~~ ~~blue~~ ~~book~~

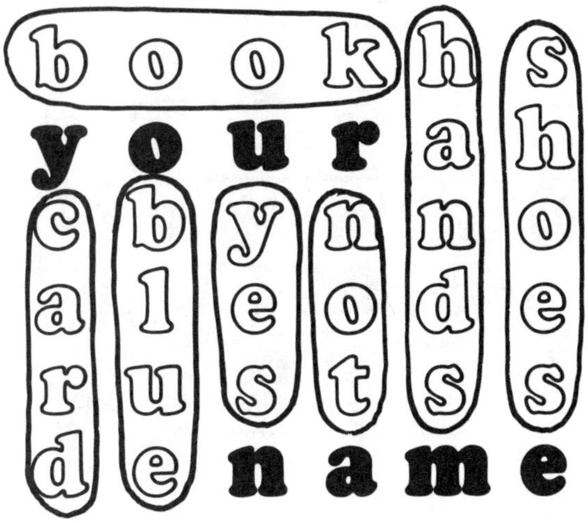

Now, find the mystery answer. Color it **purple** and write it on the line below.

your name

Page 57

What has legs but cannot walk?

1. Find and color these words **red**.

~~five~~ ~~light~~ ~~twenty~~ ~~chair~~
~~lamps~~ ~~night~~

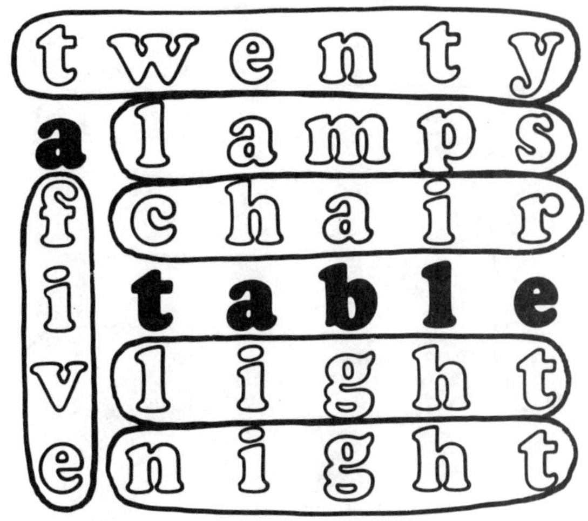

2. Now, find the mystery answer. Color it **blue** and write it on the line below

a table

Page 58

What is the best thing to put into a pie?

1. Find and color these words **yellow**.

~~nose~~ ~~arm~~ ~~mouth~~
~~hands~~ ~~bones~~ ~~belly~~

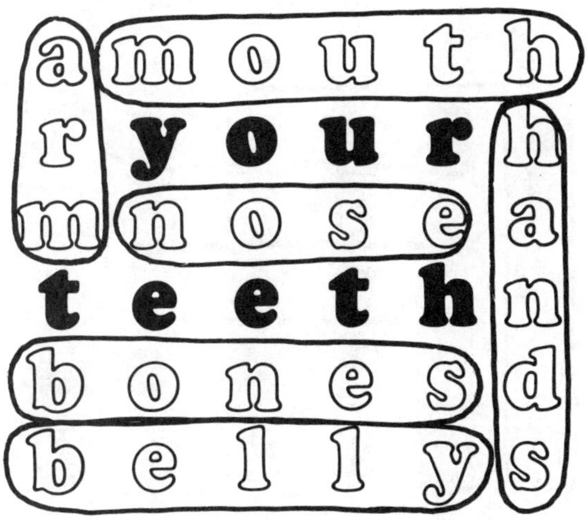

2. Now, find the mystery answer. Color it **green** and write it on the line below.

your teeth

Page 59

What runs but never walks?

1. Find and color these words **orange**.

~~wagon~~ ~~kite~~ ~~dogs~~ ~~bus~~
~~baby~~ ~~girl~~ ~~ant~~ ~~rain~~

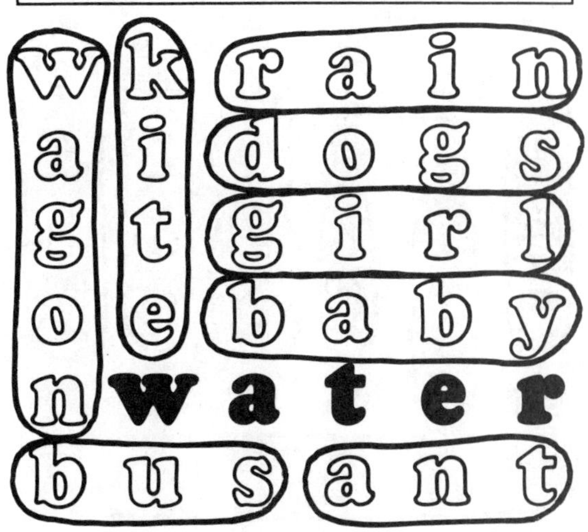

2. Now, find the mystery answer. Color it **green** and write it on the line below.

water

Page 60

Answer Key

What dog keeps the best time?

1. Find and color these words **purple**.

~~spell~~ ~~read~~ ~~add~~ ~~go~~
~~math~~ ~~lunch~~ ~~wait~~

r	e	a	d	g	o
m	a	w	a	i	t
a	l	u	n	c	h
t	w	a	t	c	h
h	s	p	e	l	l
d	o	g	a	d	d

2. Now, find the mystery answer. Color it **orange** and write it on the line below.

a watch dog

Page 61

My hair is falling out. What can I get to keep it in?

1. Find and color these words **blue**.

~~spot~~ ~~tail~~ ~~if~~ ~~socks~~
~~eggs~~ ~~wheel~~ ~~tin~~

s	p	o	t	a	e
w	h	e	e	l	g
p	a	p	e	r	g
t	t	a	i	l	s
i	i	f	b	a	g
n	s	o	c	k	s

2. Now, find the mystery answer. Color it **yellow** and write it on the line below.

a paper bag

Page 62

What has a head and a tail but no body?

1. Find and color these words **orange**.

~~trap~~ ~~ape~~ ~~pie~~ ~~trains~~
~~face~~ ~~if~~ ~~am~~ ~~dark~~ ~~day~~

f	d	a	y	t	d
a	p	i	e	r	a
c	a	i	a	a	r
e	p	f	m	p	k
a	e	c	o	i	n
t	r	a	i	n	s

2. Now, find the mystery answer. Color it **purple** and write it on the line below.

a coin

Page 63

What has hands but no feet?

1. Find and color these words **green**.

~~hands~~ ~~time~~ ~~feet~~ ~~sleep~~
~~ring~~ ~~bug~~ ~~bells~~

b	e	l	l	s	t
s	a	b	u	g	i
l	r	i	n	g	m
e	f	e	e	t	e
e	c	l	o	c	k
p	h	a	n	d	s

2. Now, find the mystery answer. Color it **yellow** and write it on the line below.

a clock

Page 64

Answer Key

Name ______________________ Word Search

Numbers

M	A	Z	T	S	I	X
T	E	N	W	X	O	P
Y	I	F	O	U	R	O
F	G	S	E	V	E	N
I	H	L	N	I	N	E
V	T	H	R	E	E	B
E	C	D	E	F	G	H

~~ONE~~ ~~TWO~~ ~~THREE~~

~~FOUR~~ ~~FIVE~~ ~~SIX~~ ~~SEVEN~~

~~EIGHT~~ ~~NINE~~ ~~TEN~~

Brainwork! How old are you? ______
Write the number word. answers will vary

Page 65

Name ______________________ Word Search

Colors

A	Y	E	L	L	O	W
B	R	O	W	N	R	E
R	B	B	H	O	A	B
E	E	L	I	C	N	L
D	A	U	T	U	G	A
G	R	E	E	N	E	C
P	U	R	P	L	E	K

~~WHITE~~ ~~GREEN~~ ~~RED~~

~~BLACK~~ ~~BLUE~~ ~~ORANGE~~

~~BROWN~~ ~~PURPLE~~ ~~YELLOW~~

Extra Word! What animal is brown? b e a r

Page 66

Name ______________________ Word Search

Farm Animals

J	S	H	E	E	P	E
U	B	F	Q	C	O	W
G	O	A	T	H	N	A
H	O	R	S	E	Y	L
O	K	M	O	N	E	L
G	H	E	C	A	L	F
M	I	R	B	U	L	L

~~COW~~ ~~CALF~~ ~~PONY~~

~~HOG~~ ~~SHEEP~~ ~~BULL~~

~~HORSE~~ ~~HEN~~ ~~GOAT~~

Extra Word! Who takes care of the farm animals?
f a r m e r

Page 67

Name ______________________ Word Search

Body Parts

F	O	O	T	L	B	A
N	J	H	E	A	D	L
V	P	A	Z	M	O	L
B	K	N	O	S	E	E
E	X	D	U	F	Y	G
A	R	M	W	H	E	P
R	C	E	S	K	I	N

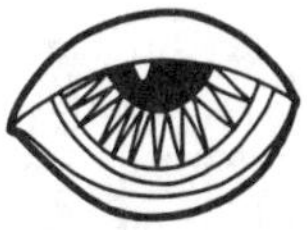

~~HAND~~ ~~FOOT~~ ~~HEAD~~

~~ARM~~ ~~LEG~~ ~~EYE~~

~~EAR~~ ~~NOSE~~ ~~SKIN~~

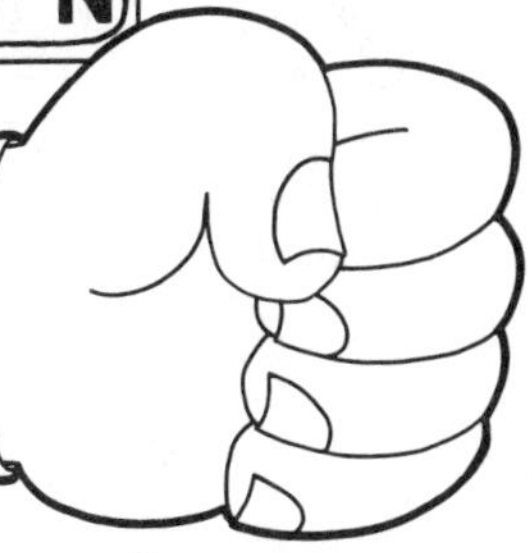

Brainwork! What word is a kind of ball? f o o t ball
or handball

Page 68

Answer Key

Name ______________________ Word Search

Zoo Animals

S	H	T	B	E	A	R
E	I	W	X	T	L	B
A	P	E	L	I	O	N
L	P	A	T	G	F	N
M	O	N	K	E	Y	V
A	Z	E	B	R	A	H
Y	I	P	A	N	D	A

~~TIGER~~ ~~SEAL~~ ~~HIPPO~~
~~LION~~ ~~BEAR~~ ~~PANDA~~
~~MONKEY~~ ~~ZEBRA~~ ~~APE~~

Brainwork! Find two animals with stripes.
zebra, tiger

Page 69

Name ______________________ Word Search

Clothing

Z	A	S	H	O	E	L
F	S	K	D	H	A	T
S	H	I	R	T	X	M
O	O	R	E	L	C	R
C	R	T	S	W	O	K
K	T	Y	S	N	A	P
E	S	P	A	N	T	S

~~SKIRT~~
~~HAT~~ ~~COAT~~
~~PANTS~~ ~~SHORTS~~
~~DRESS~~ ~~SOCK~~ ~~SHOE~~ ~~SHIRT~~

Brainwork! Find two words that rhyme.
shirt, skirt

Page 70

Name ______________________ Word Search

Things That Go

T	R	U	C	K	P	L
B	O	A	T	J	O	M
I	C	E	R	C	A	R
K	K	X	A	B	N	B
J	E	T	I	U	C	I
D	T	F	N	S	G	K
T	R	P	L	A	N	E

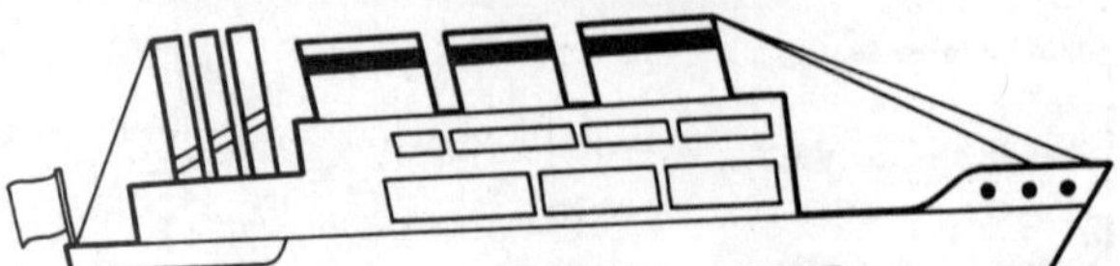

~~CAR~~ ~~TRAIN~~ ~~BOAT~~
~~BIKE~~ ~~BUS~~ ~~ROCKET~~
~~TRUCK~~ ~~PLANE~~ ~~JET~~

Brainwork! Which would you like to drive? answers will vary

Page 71

Name ______________________ Word Search

Outdoors

O	B	R	O	C	K	G
L	I	T	T	E	R	R
P	R	A	R	K	H	A
A	D	D	E	N	I	S
T	C	R	E	E	K	S
H	F	L	O	W	E	R
A	N	I	M	A	L	T

~~TREE~~ ~~GRASS~~ ~~ROCK~~
~~CREEK~~ ~~PATH~~ ~~HIKE~~
~~BIRD~~ ~~FLOWER~~ ~~ANIMAL~~

Extra Word! What does not belong outdoors?
litter

Page 72

Answer Key

Name ______________________ Word Search

Feelings

S	I	L	L	Y	S	G
T	E	L	L	G	A	R
H	I	B	O	L	D	I
A	C	O	W	A	E	N
P	R	O	U	D	N	S
P	O	H	U	R	T	H
Y	P	E	N	J	O	Y

HAPPY
SAD HURT
JOY PROUD BOLD
SILLY GLAD SHY

Extra Word! When I feel happy, I grin

Page 73

Name ______________________ Word Search

Birds

M	D	U	C	K	B	K
D	O	T	S	G	U	R
C	V	J	O	U	G	O
R	E	A	G	L	E	B
O	A	Y	E	L	L	I
W	T	T	W	R	E	N
P	P	A	R	R	O	T

WREN CROW JAY
EAGLE DOVE DUCK
GULL PARROT ROBIN

Extra Word! What rhymes with hug? bug

Page 74

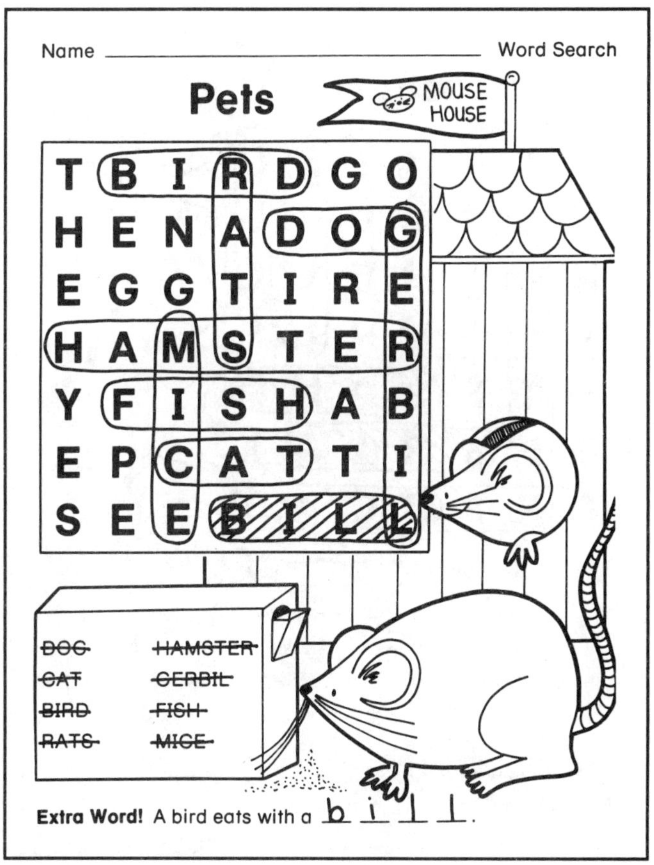

Name ______________________ Word Search

Pets

T	B	I	R	D	G	O
H	E	N	A	D	O	G
E	G	G	T	I	R	E
H	A	M	S	T	E	R
Y	F	I	S	H	A	B
E	P	C	A	T	T	I
S	E	E	B	I	L	L

DOG HAMSTER
CAT GERBIL
BIRD FISH
RATS MICE

Extra Word! A bird eats with a bill.

Page 75

Name ______________________ Word Search

Weather

P	S	F	H	A	I	L
C	L	O	U	D	Y	M
B	E	G	S	N	O	W
O	E	U	R	S	R	T
O	T	O	A	U	N	O
T	B	W	I	N	D	Y
S	O	W	N	Y	E	T

SNOW SLEET
RAIN SUN
HAIL FOG
CLOUDY WINDY

Extra Word! What do you wear on a rainy day? boots

Page 76

Answer Key

Name ______________________ Word Search

Sports Action

J	R	U	N	K	I	C
U	I	S	W	I	M	X
M	D	K	A	C	K	R
G	E	A	J	K	G	I
R	U	T	J	U	M	P
U	M	E	Z	J	O	G
H	O	P	S	W	I	N

~~RUN~~ ~~KICK~~ ~~SKATE~~ ~~RIDE~~
~~HOP~~ ~~JUMP~~ ~~SWIM~~ ~~JOG~~

Brainwork! Which do you like to do best? answers will vary

Page 77

Name ______________________ Word Search

Food

D	O	C	P	L	U	M
S	T	A	M	I	L	K
A	B	R	E	A	D	S
P	O	R	A	M	P	T
P	A	O	T	O	E	O
L	T	T	N	Y	A	V
E	C	H	E	E	S	E

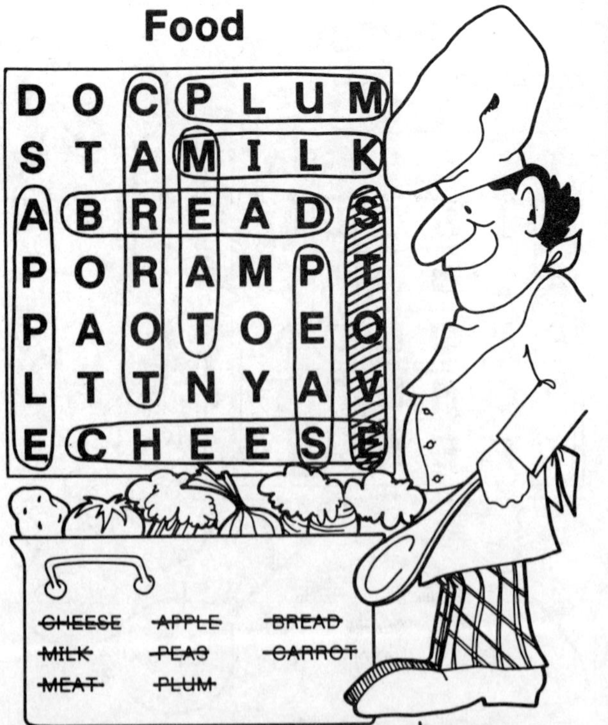

~~CHEESE~~ ~~APPLE~~ ~~BREAD~~
~~MILK~~ ~~PEAS~~ ~~CARROT~~
~~MEAT~~ ~~PLUM~~

Extra Word! What can help you cook? s t o v e

Page 78

Name ______________________ Word Search

Insects

F	W	Z	T	M	P	I
L	A	D	Y	B	U	G
E	S	N	T	E	O	X
A	P	B	E	E	L	A
F	O	M	O	T	H	N
M	M	P	F	L	Y	T
D	H	O	N	E	Y	R

~~BEE~~ ~~FLEA~~
~~MOTH~~ ~~LADYBUG~~
~~FLY~~ ~~ANT~~
~~WASP~~ ~~BEETLE~~

Extra Word! Something sticky is h o n e y

Page 79

Name ______________________ Word Search

Seashore

F	I	S	H	T	B	G
N	O	P	M	L	A	U
R	W	S	H	E	L	L
P	A	I	L	R	L	L
L	T	F	S	A	N	D
T	E	S	H	I	P	X
C	R	A	B	O	A	T

~~BALL~~ ~~SHELL~~ ~~BOAT~~
~~WATER~~ ~~CRAB~~ ~~PAIL~~
~~FISH~~ ~~SAND~~ ~~GULL~~

Extra Word! What is bigger than a boat? s h i p

Page 80

Answer Key

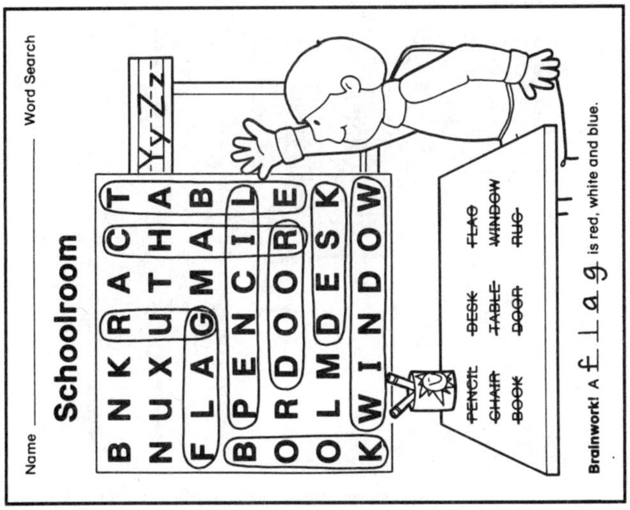

Page 81

Page 82

Page 83

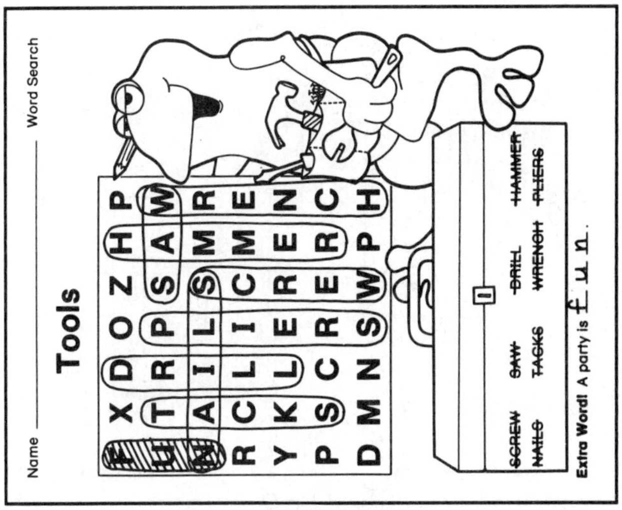

Page 84

Page 85

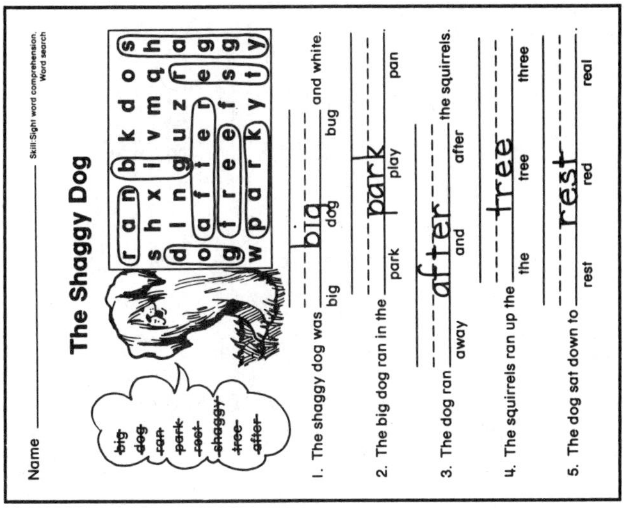

Page 86

Answer Key

The Little Kitten

Name ______________ Skill: Sight word comprehension, Word search

~~little~~ ~~cute~~ ~~keep~~ ~~kittens~~ ~~six~~ ~~name~~ ~~soft~~ ~~white~~

s	o	f	t	c	u	t	e
l	i	t	t	l	e	v	t
e	x	a	w	k	z	d	n
k	i	t	t	e	n	s	a
w	h	i	t	e	b	i	m
m	u	c	f	p	k	x	e

1. Pat's cat had six kittens. (kittens kite keep)
2. Pat likes the little white one. (like little look)
3. The little kitten is cute and soft. (can cut cute)
4. Pat will keep the white kitten. (kite keep kitten)
5. She will name it Snowball. (name man not)

Page 87

Good Friends

Name ______________ Skill: Sight word comprehension, Word search

~~rabbit~~ ~~carrot~~ ~~hungry~~ ~~bug~~ ~~eat~~ ~~friends~~ ~~little~~ ~~sits~~

f	r	i	e	n	d	s	c
p	x	t	s	i	t	s	a
o	h	u	n	g	r	y	r
l	i	t	t	l	e	b	r
s	e	i	c	t	a	u	o
r	a	b	b	i	t	g	t

1. The rabbit has a good carrot. (clean carrot came)
2. It is a hungry rabbit. (hopped have hungry)
3. A little red bug sits on the street. (said sits sad)
4. The bug and rabbit are friends. (find flower friends)
5. They will eat the carrot. (eat eye eel)

Page 88

Baby Frogs

Name ______________ Skill: Sight word comprehension, Word search

~~found~~ ~~frogs~~ ~~pond~~ ~~jar~~ ~~tadpoles~~ ~~them~~ ~~watch~~ ~~grow~~

b	p	f	t	h	e	m	f
j	o	o	g	r	o	w	r
a	n	u	d	v	k	y	o
r	d	n	x	g	z	q	g
t	a	d	p	o	l	e	s
h	w	a	t	c	h	o	u

1. Kim went to the pond. (pan pond found)
2. She found some tadpoles. (tadpoles the found)
3. Kim put them in a jar. (jump jar far)
4. She will watch them grow. (grow frogs green)
5. They will grow into frogs. (found far frogs)

Page 89

Something Good

Name ______________ Skill: Sight word comprehension, Word search

~~cake~~ ~~come~~ ~~hole~~ ~~eat~~ ~~cat~~ ~~little~~ ~~mouse~~ ~~smell~~

e	a	t	l	c	o	m	e
r	h	p	i	h	z	o	u
c	k	b	t	o	x	u	c
a	f	x	t	l	v	s	a
t	m	q	l	e	c	e	k
g	s	m	e	l	l	j	e

1. The mouse can smell something good. (smell small came)
2. The mouse is out of its hole. (have hole had)
3. The mouse sees a little bit of cake. (cat cake came)
4. It does not see the cat. (cat cake came)
5. The mouse will eat the cake. (cat came eat)

Page 90

Tim's Bird

Name ______________ Skill: Sight word comprehension, Word search

~~bird~~ ~~hand~~ ~~cage~~ ~~blue~~ ~~hi~~ ~~little~~ ~~say~~ ~~sit~~

m	l	y	b	u	h	c	k
s	i	t	i	c	a	g	e
r	t	o	r	v	n	w	s
s	t	j	d	z	d	v	f
a	l	q	x	b	l	u	e
y	e	g	p	x	h	i	b

1. Tim has a pet bird. (blue bird band)
2. The bird is little and blue. (blue bird band)
3. The bird can sit on his hand. (hello had hand)
4. Tim's bird can say, "Hi!" (sat say sit)
5. The bird lives in a cage. (cage came cake)

Page 91

My Funny Pet

Name ______________ Skill: Sight word comprehension, Word search

~~eat~~ ~~farm~~ ~~fat~~ ~~pig~~ ~~food~~ ~~mud~~ ~~funny~~ ~~roll~~

b	f	u	n	n	y	g	r
f	s	k	p	t	f	v	o
o	j	c	i	h	a	e	l
o	w	p	g	o	t	a	l
d	f	a	r	m	x	t	k
y	d	q	m	u	d	z	m

1. My pig is big and fat. (farm fat fun)
2. My pig is on a farm. (farm fun fat)
3. It likes to eat food. (fat eat mud)
4. It likes to roll in the mud. (roll rat for)
5. I love my funny pet. (food run funny)

Page 92

Answer Key

Page 93

Name ______ Skill: Sight word comprehension, Word search

A Surprise

~~big~~ ~~all~~ ~~birthday~~ ~~door~~ ~~friends~~ ~~party~~ ~~great~~ ~~surprise~~

b i r t h d a y
p a r t y o b x
f z a l l o l h
g r e a t r g k
f r i e n d s n
s u r p r i s e

1. Pam peeked around the door. (door / do / doing)
2. She saw a big surprise. (some / surprise / say)
3. It was a birthday party. (party / pan / pat)
4. All of her friends were there. (find / four / friends)
5. It was a great party. (great / green / doing)

Page 94

Name ______ Skill: Sight word comprehension, Word search

A Duck Family

~~baby~~ ~~big~~ ~~ducks~~ ~~brown~~ ~~mother~~ ~~swim~~ ~~pond~~ ~~yellow~~

k b r o w n y g
q y m o t h e r
b p c j w b l x
a o s w i m l b
b n v d z f o i
y d u c k s w g

1. Two ducks are in the pond. (pond / brown / down)
2. Mother duck is big and brown. (brown / down / duck)
3. A little duck is yellow. (yellow / yes / swim)
4. The ducks like to swim and splash. (swim / star / sky)
5. The baby duck will swim with its mother. (moon / mother / many)

Page 95

Name ______ Skill: Sight word comprehension, Word search

Fun at the Park

~~ball~~ ~~after~~ ~~bat~~ ~~friends~~ ~~game~~ ~~fun~~ ~~park~~ ~~school~~

b a t f p f u n
a f r i e n d s
l t d z q e y g
l e v p a r k a
j r s m x b r m
s c h o o l k e

1. After school, Joe went to the park. (park / after / pat)
2. He took his bat and ball. (bit / bat / bet)
3. He met his friends in the park. (find / friends / after)
4. They played a game. (game / park / good)
5. They had fun in the park. (bat / after / fun)

Page 96

Name ______ Skill: Sight word comprehension, Word search

Bozo Bear

~~ball~~ ~~bear~~ ~~spin~~ ~~circus~~ ~~live~~ ~~dance~~ ~~people~~ ~~tricks~~

d a n c e a j p
f c i r c u s e
b s p i n d k o
e g r l i v e p
a l c w b a l l
r t r i c k s e

1. Bozo Bear lives in a circus. (circus / clap / cat)
2. He can do many tricks. (tricks / roll / this)
3. Bozo Bear can spin and dance. (don't / bear / dance)
4. He can roll on a big ball. (ball / roll / band)
5. People like to see Bozo. (Roll / People / Dance)

Page 97

Name ______ Skill: Sight word comprehension, Word search

Trip to the Moon

~~rocks~~ ~~far~~ ~~man~~ ~~fly~~ ~~moon~~ ~~rocket~~ ~~up~~ ~~walk~~

m a n c g w f n
r g f a r a l y
o z u v q l y m
c c p k x k v o
k r o c k e t o
s j l e m a r n

1. The man will go in the rocket. (rich / rocket / rock)
2. The rocket will fly to the moon. (fly / far / fish)
3. The moon is far away. (farm / fast / far)
4. The man will walk on the moon. (was / want / walk)
5. He will look at the rocks. (rocks / far / ran)

Page 98

Name ______ Skill: Sight word comprehension, Word search

A New Toy

~~balloon~~ ~~bear~~ ~~brown~~ ~~hug~~ ~~little~~ ~~soft~~ ~~toy~~

s o f t b r z l
v d s m r b f i
b a l l o o n t
e k h o w q x t
a c u v n y g l
r j g e t o y e

1. I have a new toy. (toy / the / to)
2. It is a little brown bear. (beg / bear / best)
3. I love to give it a hug. (have / had / hug)
4. It is soft and brown. (so / saw / soft)
5. My bear has a little balloon. (bring / balloon / big)

Answer Key

Name ______________ Skill: Sight word comprehension. Word search

Visit to the Doctor

arm
doctor
fell
hurt
play
running
street
fix

h	f	e	l	l	e	k	s
q	i	x	y	h	u	r	t
y	x	d	o	c	t	o	r
a	i	p	l	a	y	d	e
r	u	n	n	i	n	g	e
m	z	b	u	j	z	s	t

1. Ted was running down the street.
hurt street said
2. He fell and hurt his arm.
am arm at
3. Ted went to see a doctor.
doctor don't doing
4. The doctor will fix Ted's arm.
fox fell fix
5. Ted cannot play a game.
play played playing

Page 99

Name ______________ Skill: Sight word comprehension. Word search

Sammy Seal

bark
circus
seal
horn
play
have
clap
trick

c	i	b	q	h	o	r	n
i	h	a	v	e	y	s	t
r	d	r	c	s	w	e	r
c	j	k	l	p	c	a	i
u	a	z	a	f	s	l	c
s	k	m	p	l	a	y	k

1. Come to see the circus.
clap circus come
2. You will see Sammy the seal.
see sees seal
3. Sammy will do a trick for you.
truck trick this
4. Sammy can play the horn.
horn have had
5. Sammy can clap and bark.
bark big bad

Page 100

Name ______________ Skill: Sight word comprehension. Word search

A Letter for Fran

away
every
for
letter
hear
lives
week
from

w	e	e	k	l	e	g	f
o	s	l	e	t	t	e	r
y	f	o	r	d	u	a	o
e	v	e	r	y	p	w	m
z	l	i	v	e	s	a	e
h	e	a	r	k	z	y	s

1. Fran got a letter today.
let little letter
2. The letter was from her grandmother.
four from far
3. Fran likes to hear from her grandmother.
her hear had
4. Her grandmother lives far away.
away every and
5. Her grandmother writes every week.
walk we week

Page 101

Name ______________ Skill: Sight word comprehension. Word search

Hide-and-Seek

turtle
grass
pond
find
after
dog
away
get

a	w	a	y	g	t	r	g
f	y	t	u	r	t	l	e
t	j	a	d	a	f	o	t
e	r	e	o	s	i	i	z
r	c	x	g	s	n	i	g
p	o	n	d	k	d	s	y

1. A turtle came out of the pond.
pond hid dog
2. The turtle hid in the grass.
good grass dog
3. A big dog came to find it.
find bad hid
4. The dog did not get the turtle.
good dog get
5. The dog went away.
after away and

Page 102

Name ______________ Skill: Sight word comprehension. Word search

Bobo

circus
clap
face
funny
laugh
tricks
like

l	f	a	c	e	c	c	f
i	l	v	i	q	l	l	r
k	a	e	r	k	o	a	i
e	u	g	c	t	w	p	c
x	g	f	u	n	n	y	k
w	h	m	s	j	z	m	s

1. Bobo is a funny clown.
clown clap circus
2. He works in a circus.
clown clap circus
3. He likes to make people laugh.
laugh like little
4. He does funny tricks.
trucks tricks funny
5. He has a funny face.
fat face funny

Page 103

Name ______________ Skill: Sight word comprehension. Word search

The Little Bee

cat
good
little
grass
looked
up
sky
went

k	g	r	a	s	s	f	l
l	o	o	k	e	d	e	i
r	o	m	x	j	c	y	t
b	d	u	p	t	a	d	t
w	e	n	t	w	t	m	l
s	u	l	s	k	y	v	e

1. The cat sat down in the grass.
good grass get
2. The cat looked at the bee.
little liked looked
3. The little bee went up.
will went where
4. The bee went up and up.
up sun to
5. The bee went up in the sky.
something said sky

Page 104